Cycling the Islands

P.E.I. and The Magdalen Islands

Campbell Webster

BREAKWATER

Breakwater
100 Water Street
P.O. Box 2188
St. John's, Newfoundland
A1C 6E6

Photographs on cover and throughout book courtesy of Sunset Bicycle Tours.

Maps by Angela King-Harris.

The Publisher acknowledges the financial contribution of The Canada Council which has helped make this publication possible.

Canadian Cataloguing in Publication Data
Webster, Campbell

    Cycling the Islands
    ISBN 0-920911-87-0

1. Prince Edward Island—Description and travel—Guide-books. 2. Iles-de-Madeleine (Quebec)—Description and travel —Guide-books. 3. Bicycle touring—Prince Edward Island—Guide-books. 4. Bicycle touring—Quebec (Province)—Iles-de-la-Madeleine—Guide-books. I. Title.

GV1046.C2W42 1990   917.1704'4   C90-097544-X

CONTENTS

WHY P.E.I.?

Nationally acclaimed Island potter Peter Jansons (despite the fact he refers to himself as just a 'little famous') once said to me, "What I find interesting about visitors to the Island is not why they come 'from away' in the first place, but what brings them back to the Island a second and third time." Implicit in his observations is the fact that many visitors to the Island do return time and time again. Unlike many vacation spots you may have visited, the Island is not just experienced, remembered, and filed away with other vacations. Rather, it quickly becomes part of you, like an old friend that you miss, a relationship that you want to nurture and renew. It is the personal warmth of the Island and the subtly safe, removed tranquillity of its beautiful landscape and shores that make you long to return. It also happens to be great for cycling. If you had to design an Island with the express intention of creating a spring/summer/fall cycling haven, P.E.I. would be it.

Over the past few summers, my partner and I have led over three hundred and fifty cyclists on package tours of the Island. I became so enamoured with cycling the Island through my work that I even spent my days off cycling with my good friend and master storyteller, Erskine Smith. Late one hot July evening in 1987, I realized something extraordinary about the Island's ability to coax me and so many others into returning time and time again. That day, a group of twelve cyclists and I had cycled a short twenty-seven miles north from Charlottetown and along the striking North Shore to our destination, Brackley Beach. Along the way we were stopped no less than three times by Islanders who inquired about our well-being and whether we needed directions. Their unsolicited concern and friendliness amazed our group and, as it turns out, is typical of Islanders. After an afternoon of windsurfing, sailing and generally enjoying the ocean, and an evening at a typically sumptuous lobster supper, a friend and I took a walk on the grounds of the historical North Shore ocean resort Shaw's Hotel, run by fourth generation owner, Robbie Shaw.

The sky was clear and bright, and at first nothing but the gentle crashing of the ocean and swaying trees broke the silence. But after a while we noticed another sound: a deep, expansive rumbling that seemed to envelop us; the muffled thunder that accompanies the Aurora Borealis or Northern Lights. We lay down in a farmer's field that was lying fallow and watched the swimming flashes of colour move across the sky until we fell asleep in the warm salt air. I thought of the Islanders who had stopped to greet us during the day, the enveloping serenity that is the Island, and I realized that it would be part of my life forever.

As you cycle the routes suggested in this guide, or explore the Island on your own, you will no doubt discover your own relationship to the Island and its people. This guide has been written with the intention of not only helping you plan a cycling vacation, but also to help you enjoy the many other experiences that are the Island. From deep-sea fishing, champagne harbour cruises, the musical *Anne of Green Gables*, historic churches, hundreds of brightly painted wooden gabled farm houses, endless uncrowded beaches, artisan galleries, to fiddling festivals, the Island has a lot to offer and I have tried to give you some information on those you will encounter on your route. You will also find that in the Recommended Tours in this guide you have an option of camping, staying in traditional farm tourist homes or resort hotels. But more on how to plan your own tour later. For now, welcome to the Island; it definitely welcomes you, knowing you will return a second and third time. Most people from 'away' do.

Anglo Rustico, PEI (Day B)

GENERAL INFORMATION

 ## Roads/Terrain

Topography

If you were playing a word association game and the word 'Island' came up, you might, being a devout cyclist, counter with the word 'flat'. While it's true you won't find any snow-capped mountain ranges on the Island, do not expect it to be one long counter top. It is generally quite flat along the shores, but also considerably more windy. Most inland routes have some hills and although very few Island hills should take you more than ten minutes to cycle, they tend to come in rapid succession. If the most feared words of the cyclist are "Lunch is just over that mountain," the most often heard words of the Island cyclist are "Lunch is just over those hills—all five of them." They are not backbreakers, but do not be deceived by their quality, or you may be humbled by their quantity.

Traffic

The Island has the distinction of having the highest mileage of roads per capita of any province in Canada. For this reason, you can usually get from any given point A to any given point B in a number of ways. This is ideal for the cyclist who wants to avoid the seven busy routes and still cycle to those areas that everybody seems to want to go to. You will find that this guide's suggested routes bypass as many of the busy routes as possible.

If you are setting out on your own to a popular destination you might try the following method in selecting quieter roads: on your Visitors Map (available from the Prince Edward Island Department of Tourism) select the direct route to your destination. These routes, particularly in Queens County, will have a fair amount of tourist traffic. Then choose the route YOU will take; you should have no trouble finding one beside or near the main route. For example, the most direct route to Brackley Beach from Charlottetown is Route 15 which, in the summer, is quite busy, but Union Road and a quiet portion of Route 6 run right beside it and are virtually untravelled. You might see fifteen to twenty cars in the twenty-seven miles to your destination.

Generally, you will find the most traffic in Queens County, some traffic in Kings County, and very little in Prince County. The routes you can count on almost always being busy between July 1 and Labour Day are Routes 1, 2, 3, 4, 6, 13, and 15, particularly in Queens County, and on sunny days. (People avoid travel to beaches on rainy days for some reason.) In early spring and fall, almost anywhere on the Island is lightly travelled with the exception of Routes 1 and 2. Do not assume from this that Prince County is automatically the best cycling territory—there are reasons why Queens and Kings Counties are busier—and depending on what you are looking for, all of the three counties are well worth visiting.

Quality of Roads

With the exception of the main routes mentioned above, most Island roads are quite narrow and have little or no shoulders. This is usually not a problem, owing to the extremely light traffic. If, however, you prefer to have a nice, comfortable shoulder all to your very own, you should cycle in the National Park. The National Park roads are also lightly travelled and have wide, well-maintained shoulders. The National Park features the striking red cliffs and the dune-guarded white beaches of Queens County's North Shore, and is ideal for a day trip.

As you seek out your alternates to the main routes, you may occasionally run across dirt roads, usually portions of routes that have not been or never will be paved. Unless there has been a torrential downpour in the last couple of days, they are generally well maintained enough for cycling and do not have too many potholes, too much gravel or mud. Often they can take you to secluded ocean front scenery and other 'finds' that you would not otherwise come across, as is the case with Route 243 north, off Route 6 near South Rustico.

New London, PEI (Day C)

 Tourist Information

When you arrive on the Island, one of your first stops should be at one of the Visitors Information Centres, which are located at both ferry terminals and in Charlottetown in the Royalty Mall on University Avenue. They offer an outstanding assortment of publications and services, are extremely well-staffed, well-informed and friendly. Tourism is the second largest industry on the

Island, and the Government's commitment to it is therefore extensive. You may also phone Tourism toll-free if you live in the Canadian Maritime Provinces (1-800-565-7421), Ontario, Quebec and Newfoundland (1-800-565-0243), or the Eastern United States (1-800-565-9060).

Whether you phone before your trip, or drop by when you come to the Island, you should get a copy of the Visitors Guide, a comprehensive, award-winning publication. You would be wise to get a copy before you come to the Island. The Visitors Guide includes everything from a county by county camping and accommodations listing of most places to stay on the Island, to a highly detailed map of the Island, a listing and description of sixty-seven major Island attractions, a brief history of the Island, and descriptions of sixty ongoing Island activities, as well as the Places to Eat Guide. The Visitors Guide is a must for any visitor to the Island and is free of charge.

While at the Visitors Information Centre you should also pick up any other pamphlets that suit your particular area of interest. Most tourist outfits on the Island publish a pamphlet, so your choices of information will be quite broad. Try to select from the Visitors Guide what you want to know more about, and then find the pamphlet relevant to your area of interest. You will usually find something. They also carry publications from the various package cycling tour operations. You would also be smart to take advantage of the Visitors Information Centres' free accommodation booking service. A battery of Tourism personnel monitor the availability of most accommodations in a large chalkboard-filled room, and will book rooms for you as you wait. This is particularly useful if you have planned your own tour in advance, as the Visitors Information Centre will help find accommodations in the areas you wish to stay overnight.

If you are planning on cycling to the Magdalen Islands, make sure you pick up the Magdalen Island

Tourist Guide, which includes a map of the Magdalens, and the C.T.M.A. Ferry Schedule to the Magdalens. Both these publications are available at the Prince Edward Island Visitors Information Centres. The toll-free numbers for tourist information in the Magdalen Islands are 873-2015 (from Montreal), 1-800-361-5405 (elsewhere in Quebec), 1-800-361-6490 (from Ontario and the Atlantic Provinces), 1-800-443-7000 (from the Eastern United States.)

 ## Accommodations

There are basically four types of accommodations available on the Island: campgrounds, tourist or farm tourist homes, resorts, and motel/hotels. 1989 prices range from $8.00 for a campsite to $90.00 for a room at the Charlottetown Hotel. If you are cycling in Queens County to major destinations along the North Shore, you can pretty well have your choice of campgrounds, farm tourist homes, or resorts. Otherwise, farm tourist homes are usually your best bet; many Islanders across all three counties open up their homes as tourist homes in the summer. They rarely charge more than $40.00 for bed and breakfast, are quite clean, and are often brightly painted farm houses located near the shore. All of the tourist homes that we have encountered on our tours have been very accommodating to cyclists. Best of all, the owners are usually very warm and personable, exuding typical Island hospitality and concern for your well-being. A personal favourite: Lyndon Cove Farm Tourist Home, run by Buddy and Helen MacEwen and located near Stanley Bridge overlooking the Cavendish Capes. Buddy and Helen's quick wit, attention to detail, and beautifully located family farm has made their farm a regular stop for our tours for seven years. They will tell you a story or twelve, educate you about the history of their family and their part of the Island, and generally make you feel like you have been there for years.

The Visitors Guide lists most tourist homes by one of the three counties: Prince, Queens and Kings. All of the Visitors Guide listings have been approved by Tourism, so you can usually count on any accommodation you find in it. However, because of the wide circulation of the Visitors Guide and the popularity of Queens County tourist homes in the summer, you would be smart to reserve rooms in advance. It could be quite depressing to cycle forty miles to a beautiful beach front tourist home to find nothing but the beach left to sleep on. Then again, it could be quite refreshing on a warm, moonlit Island night.

 Seasons

The Island is suitable for cycling from June until mid-October, with the peak season being between July 1 and Labour Day. There are a variety of factors you will want to consider in choosing when you come to the Island.

June
The month of June can be unpredictable, but generally you will find the days are warm, the nights are cool and the ocean is warm enough only for the particularly brave. (There are Islanders who swim from April to November on the relatively warm South Shore, but that is probably a result of the same psychology that makes people plunge into Canadian lakes on New Year's Day.) June is quiet and you will find that even the popular destinations are virtually deserted. The expansive, red-cliffed Cavendish Capes can be an exhilarating ride in June, with miles of ocean front, time sculpted sandstone cliffs, and small villages all to yourself. In early June, most of the larger commercialized tourist attractions will not be open, and fewer accommodations will be open. (Those that are

open will almost certainly have space.) By the third week of June, most summer restaurants, lobster suppers, theatres and hotels have opened for the summer, and this may be an ideal time to cycle the Island: the days are getting warmer, accommodation availability is still good, and most of the visitors services and attractions are open.

Summer

From July 1 until Labour Day, the Island is in full swing. The days and nights are warm, and by the second week of July the ocean water is heating up to comfortable temperatures. (By mid-August it can reach 20 degrees celsius.) The North Shore between Brackley Beach and Cavendish Beach will be quite busy and thus campsites and accommodations can be hard to find. Cycling on hot, sunny days can be fantastic during this time, with lots to see and do along the way. You will also run into many of your cycling brethren. If you are keen on cycling mostly along the shoreline, this is a great time to do it: no matter where you are on the Island, there is usually a beach that is easily accessible by bicycle. You will rarely cycle more than five miles along the shoreline without having the option (or the overwhelming desire) to go swimming.

Fall

Fall cycling on the Island allows you to see the Island in a different light than summer visitors. The Island slows down and takes a breather from its active summer, and Islanders will be relaxed and have more time on their hands to spend with you. You will be hard-pressed to find activities like beach front theme parks and mini-putt courses. Some activities you will still be able to enjoy are the Charlottetown Harbour Cruises, the Charlottetown Festival Theatre, sailing, deep-sea fishing, and most historical buildings, such as Province House—the 'Cradle of Confederation'. Off-season rates apply in most hotels, and availability is no problem. It can get quite cold at night and the ocean stops being hospitable by mid-September. Long fall shadows make cycling inland past harvesting farmers particularly serene. Harbourfront villages, such as Victoria on the South Shore, are a good bet in fall, giving you an opportunity to taste historical Island village life. Generally, cycling on the Island in the fall, like the spring, can be a quite private experience with most of the advantages of the summer still available.

Southwest River, PEI (Day C)

TRIP PREPARATION

Now that you have made some decisions about when and where you would like to go on the Island (based on this guide's chapter on General Information and the Visitors Guide), it's time to decide how you are going to get to the Island, what type of bicycle and accessories you will need (whether you will use your own or rent one on the Island), what reservations you will need to make, how far you want to cycle daily, and what general and specific Island bicycle safety you will need to keep in mind. That is what is called trip preparation. The more you prepare, the less likely you are to run into problems en route. Read on. Much of the following information is specific to the Island.

 ## Getting to the Island

There are three different ways for you and your bicycle to get to the Island; driving or cycling on to one of the two ferries, by train, or by plane. Each has its advantages and disadvantages relevant to season, cost, and relative hassle.

Ferries
There are two ferry services to the Island offered during the cycling season: Northumberland Ferries, crossing regularly between Caribou, Nova Scotia and Wood Islands, Prince Edward Island; and Marine Atlantic, crossing regularly between Cape Tormentine, New

Brunswick and Borden, Prince Edward Island. Extreme weather conditions sometimes cause the temporary suspension of both services, but this is rare in the summer. Both are relatively inexpensive, particularly if you are cycling on, owing to the fact that they are government subsidized.

1989 prices for Northumberland Ferries are $10.00 for a car, $1.50 for your bicycle (no charge if it's attached to your car), $3.10 per adult, and $1.55 for children between five and twelve. Children under five are free. In the summer they offer service leaving both terminals every 75 minutes, starting at 6 a.m. and finishing at 9:50 p.m. The Nova Scotia terminal is about 1 3/4 hours driving time from Halifax and the Island terminal is about one hour from Charlottetown. The Northumberland ferries are relatively small and cars get backed up almost every day in the summer, with weekend travellers often having to wait half the day. If you are on your bicycle, you won't have to line up, being accorded the same privilege as walk-on passengers. If you are driving, your best bet to avoid line-ups is to listen to local radio stations for ferry information, or try to catch the *first* ferry at 6 a.m. It is early, but you will almost surely get on without a wait.

1989 prices for Marine Atlantic ferries are $6.25 per car, $1.00 per bicycle, $2.40 per adult, $1.20 for children between five and twelve, and children under five are free. In the summer, they offer service leaving both terminals every hour on the half-hour, starting at 6:30 a.m. until 11:30 p.m., with one last ferry at 1:00 a.m. The New Brunswick terminal is about one hour by car from Moncton; the Island terminal is about 45 minutes by car from Charlottetown. Marine Atlantic ferries are quite large and they put extra crossings on as traffic increases. They still have line-ups during peak weekends and other busy summer days, so you would be wise to check in advance by listening to the radio or go early in the day. If you are on your bicycle, you won't have to wait in line.

Trains

VIA has a Montreal to Moncton overnight train leaving daily at 6:40 p.m., Tuesdays excepted; from Moncton there is connecting bus service to the Island. Full fare without any sleeping accommodation is usually about 60 percent of full fare airline costs. The trip takes 21 hours and, depending on which day you go, will follow one of the two routes. Both the Ocean and the Atlantic Routes have spectacular scenery; the former following the St. Lawrence River through Quebec, the latter travelling through northeastern United States wilderness. A bike box will cost you $5.00. There are connecting trains in Montreal to the rest of Canada, as well as Amtrak service from Montreal to New York and Washington, D.C.

Planes

The two airlines that service the Island are Air Canada and Canadian and their affiliates. In the summer, there is nonstop service to Montreal, Ottawa, Toronto, Halifax, and most larger Maritime cities. There are often summer bargains to be had, usually requiring that you book thirty days in advance. In 1989, full fare return flights to Montreal, Ottawa, and Toronto ran between four and five hundred dollars. Bringing a bicycle as luggage will cost $40.00 for the round trip, with the necessary purchase of a bike bag or box costing three dollars; you might consider renting on the Island unless, like many cyclists, you have a symbiotic relationship with your bicycle. Both airlines require partial disassembly of your bicycle and adjustment of the handlebars.

**Bicycles and Accessories
Suitable to Island Cycling**

Bicycles

A touring twelve-speed bicycle with racing style handlebars is more than adequate for the Island, although almost any respectable bicycle will do, as there are no excessively long climbs and few poor roads. You will not need an extra small front sprocket or 'granny gear' for climbs on the Island, as most hills don't require snail's pace cycling. Be sure to be comfortable with your saddle before you set out as you will be having a long and close relationship with it. Our tours have found that the most comfortable saddles are women's touring saddles (they are wider). Try and stay away from extra narrow racing saddles; they are designed for more calloused residents.

A mountain bike is *not* recommended for touring, as they are considerably heavier than a touring bicycle, offer more wind resistance because of their raised handlebars, more road resistance because of their wider tires, and are not necessarily sturdier than touring bicycles. In fact, mountain bikes are of far more interest to marketing agencies than they are of use to touring cyclists. Their only advantage is that they can be more comfortable for shorter distances and day trips. If you have a mountain bike and want to bring it, you should over inflate the tires by about five pounds to decrease road resistance.

Generally, any touring twelve-speed bicycle retailing at over three hundred dollars which has a good saddle, racing handlebars, a water bottle rack, a handle-bar bag, and paniers will be sufficient for the Island.

Rentals

There are two bicycle shops in Charlottetown which offer rental and road repair service; MacQueen's Bike Shop at 430 Queen Street, and The Trail Shop at 54 Queen Street. In 1989, MacQueen's charged fifteen dollars a day, fifty dollars a week, thirty dollars for a three-day week-end, and they have a selection of most styles of bikes from BMX to eighteen-speed touring bikes. Some of their bikes are older, so make sure to select one of the better models. The Trail Shop charged twelve dollars per day, $50.00 a week, $80.00 for two weeks, $25.00 for a three-day week-end, and also has a selection of twelve-speed mountain and touring bikes. Both bike shops have complete repair services and accessories.

Accessories

Because we are in the midst of a North American cycling craze, the array of cycling accessories can be expensive and vast. Unless you are completely immersed in the craze yourself, your best bet is to choose a few essential items and resist a lot of extraneous gadgets which can often cause you more grief than advantages. (One of our more over-zealous tour members bought shoes and pedals which locked to increase pedalling efficiency. While they did just that, they sometimes would not release when he stopped. The result was somewhat comic and painful.) Accessories for your bicycle should include paniers (saddle bags), a handlebar bag with a waterproof map case which is readable while you are cycling, one or two water bottles and rack, a tool set, and a pump. A handlebar-mounted rear view mirror and safety flag are important safety features for some of the Island's narrower roads.

The paniers should be multi-pocketed for easy organization, have a low centre of gravity, and be made out of sturdy, water repellant nylon. When you pack them, try to concentrate the weight towards the bottom. Try not to use a backpack instead of paniers; the balance problems and discomfort they cause make them a poor choice for long distance cycling. The rack you mount your paniers on should be sturdy, with triangular struts and forward extensions which fasten onto the seat. A cheaper, loose rack can be very dangerous. Also, make sure that they leave you enough heel clearance to cycle.

If your bike is in good shape, it is unlikely you will have any serious breakdowns on the road on a two- or three-week trip. The most common problem is a flat tire. Still, you should make sure your tool set includes a spare tube, spare spokes (which you can carry taped to the frame), a tube repair kit, spare nuts and bolts, a *complete* set of allen keys, brake/gear cable, a vice grip, and a bicycle ratchet set.

You will not need to buy a complete cycling wardrobe to cycle the Island, although cycling shorts, gloves and/or padded handlebars will make your trip more comfortable. There are many different types of cycling shorts now available and, if you are a relatively inexperienced cyclist, they might be a good idea for a first trip. Padded cycling shorts can help you avoid any discomfort in the early part of your trip. Padded handlebars and padded cycling gloves help reduce vibration in your arms and hands and are relatively inexpensive. You will probably just need one or the other; padded handlebars have the advantage of not having to be taken on and off as do gloves, gloves have the advantage of being able to be dried at the end of a rainy day. Any pair of sturdy jogging shoes are suitable for cycling and are considerably cheaper than cycling shoes. Brightly coloured shirts and windbreakers are a good idea for visibility and should be tight fitting to cut down on wind resistance. In the summer, the Island sun can be quite bright along the ocean, where you will probably do a lot of cycling, so a hat and a good pair of anti-glare sunglasses are also recommended.

You might also consider a cycle computer, which retails for approximately fifty dollars. Distances are short on the Island, so they are not essential, but they can assist you in maintaining a good cadence, steady speed, and give you a precise indication of how far you have cycled daily and during your whole trip. Consistent cadence is particularly important as it helps maximize stamina.

New Glasgow, PEI (Near Day B)

If you're planning on camping, a lightweight (approximately three pound) tent with a rain fly and waterproof floor, a summer weight sleeping bag, a thin foam pad, and a single element canister-type butane stove are recommended. They are all compact and sufficient for summer camping on the Island. Spring/fall cyclists should bring heavier sleeping bags for the cooler evenings.

Reservations of Accommodations and Activities

Before you come to the Island, particularly in the summer, you should reserve as many accommodations in advance as possible. While the Island never seems crowded, accommodations and campsites do fill up. You can make reservations at most accommodations and campsites by phone. Two to three weeks advance time should be enough in most cases. You will find phone numbers and write-ups on most accommodations in the Visitors Guide.

If you are planning to attend one of the many summer theatres on the Island, and especially if you want to see the world famous musical *Anne of Green Gables*, you may have to book your seats well in advance to be assured of a reservation. Most of the Island theatres book reservations through the Confederation Centre Box Office (902) 566-1267.

Most other activities, like tours of historical buildings, harbour cruises, balloon rides, deep-sea fishing, and sailing can be booked with a day's notice once you arrive on the Island.

 ## Distances: How Far to Go?

There is a lot to see and enjoy on the Island in a relatively small area, so you won't have to cycle 100 kms a day just to get from place to place. For example, you can do a loop around Queens County, including much of the North Shore and South Shore, in four days of about sixty km a day. If you are a beginning cyclist, you should start with about thirty to sixty km days, planning your accommodations accordingly. More experienced cyclists probably won't want to do more than 120 km days on most of the Islands because of the many small harbours, villages, and ocean front cliffs to see along the way. If you are looking for long stretches of open country, one of your best choices would be around the perimeter beach front highways of Prince County.

Bicycle Safety on the Island

Helmets

Helmets are an essential cycling safety feature and prevent major injuries if you do fall. Racing helmets are not recommended as they are designed with lightweight qualities in mind first and safety second. One or two of our 150 tour members usually fall each summer, and the only serious injury we have ever had involved a tour member who was not wearing a helmet. So wear one! No matter how goofy you think it looks.

Bicycle Adjustment

Your bicycle should be adjusted to your needs to ensure comfort, maximize stamina, proper balance, and safety. Some key areas to adjust are the brakes (which should be aligned evenly about a half-inch from either side of the rims), the gears (which should change with precision and not cause the chain to fall off or hit the spokes; use the high-low adjustments on the derailers), handlebars (which should be high enough so that you ride with a straight back), and the seat (which should be high enough to allow one leg to be slightly bent when on a pedal in its lowest position).

Gears

You should familiarize yourself with your bicycle and its gears before you set out. An hour or two of practice on a twelve- or eighteen-speed is usually enough to become comfortable at changing gears. Generally, you should gear down before you start a climb and gear up before a descent and become comfortable with your own cruising gear for flat runs. A good cadence (revolutions of your pedals per minute) is anywhere between fifty and eighty.

Food/Water

You should keep a bag of trail mix in your handlebar bag at all times, as well as one or two easily accessible water bottles attached to your bicycle frame. Try not to wait until you are thirsty or hungry to eat or drink, as heat exhaustion and dehydration can sneak up on you, especially on windy routes by the shore. The general rule is to eat before you are hungry, and drink before you're thirsty. Alcohol during the day is a bad idea as it dehydrates you quickly and compounds the effects of hot weather.

Cycling in the Rain
When it rains, you should slow down from your regular speed and try not to stop for long periods. Stopping can cause you to get cold faster, as well as inhibiting your desire to continue. You should also use your brakes differently when your rims are wet: apply them once quickly to remove water from the rims and then apply them again. Repeat this procedure if the roads are quite wet.

Cars
Most Island motorists are quite sensitive to cyclists on the road and will usually slow down, honk their horn, and give you a wide berth when they pass you. You should still be careful on some of the busier narrow roads, particularly those leading to the beaches on the North Shore. For this reason, a mirror and safety flag are strongly recommended for Island cycling. Mirrors allow you to avoid looking over your shoulder (which causes your bicycle to sway in the direction of your movement). Flags can greatly increase visibility. Flags which protrude horizontally from your rear wheel hub are recommended over vertical ones because they do not interfere with dismounting and have more movement to catch drivers' attention.

Dogs
There are a fair number of farm dogs on the Island, most of whom like to bark at, and occasionally chase, passing cyclists. If you do not feel comfortable about dogs, do not try to outrun them (they are incredibly fast), or kick them,

or abuse them, as this will get them more excited and you are likely to fall. You should slow down, dismount, and place the bicycle between yourself and the dog. It will usually lose interest and go find something else to chase.

Accessories

One of the main causes of bicycle accidents is an object getting stuck in the wheels or pedals. You should avoid any loose straps, or hanging wires from any accessories like Walkmans or backpacks. These can be extremely dangerous, particularly during quick descents, causing you to lose complete control of the bicycle.

Orby Head, PEI (Day B)

RECOMMENDED TOURS

This guide was written with one objective in mind: to develop routes across Prince Edward Island and the Magdalens that would be ideally suited to bicycle travel. While much of the information applies to visiting the region in general, its main advantage is that it covers the entire region with the eyes and expectations of a cyclist. Daily routes start and end within reasonable distances, follow untravelled routes you would not ordinarily find, and always bring you near to a campsite and a selection of accommodations. To take maximum advantage of the information and tours outlined, you should keep the following suggestions in mind:

- Each of the Daily Itineraries connects with one or two other days in the guide. Through these connections, Recommended Tours from three days up to three weeks have been suggested in the Recommended Tours section. You will find these tours just before the Daily Itineraries. Obviously, you can combine the Daily Itineraries to design your own tour, but you will find the tours assembled in this guide are designed with the objective of visiting as much of the Island as possible. As each of the Daily Itineraries are designated by a letter, each Recommended Tour is represented by a combined sequence of letters.

- Each of the Daily Itineraries begins and ends within close proximity of accommodations and campgrounds. Depending on where you have chosen to stay for the night, you should plan where your actual daily route will end before you set out. In most of the Itineraries, I have included prompts to assist you in cycling directly to a couple of accommodations in the area. Moreover, many of the Daily Itineraries end within physical view of one or more accommodations and/or campgrounds.

- The maps included in this guide are designed to give you a sense of which region you are cycling to and from, as well as giving you a physical representation of which days you would like to select for your route. They are not designed to be used for orienteering purposes. If you wish to follow a map as you cycle, you should use the tourism maps.

- As suggested in the Trip Preparation section, this guide is designed as a complement to the Prince Edward Island and Magdalen Islands Visitors Guides and Maps. While the Daily Itineraries in this guide are thorough and can be used without maps, the tourism maps are also quite detailed and work well with this guide. The Visitors Guide also details all of the campgrounds and accommodations suggested in the daily General Route Description of this guide. You will find information on how to get copies of the Visitors Guide in the Trip Preparation section of this guide.

- While following the directions in the Daily Itineraries section, you will notice that all landmarks and turns have been measured to the tenth of a kilometre. Consequently, a cycle computer would be a great addition to your bicycle so as to assist you in knowing when to look out for attractions and turns. If, however, you choose not to use a cycle computer, you will still find that the kilometre by kilometre notation gives you a sense of the pace at which you are cycling.

- As the Daily Itineraries often follow untravelled, and sometimes poorly marked, secondary routes, it is important to read the descriptions in the following Daily Itineraries carefully. Most turns have been detailed with at least two landmarks (including corner stores, gas stations and churches), so if there have been any changes since this guide went to press you should be able to find your way via at least one landmark, road sign, etc. I have noted the location of many of the churches for this purpose, as churches tend to be more permanent than corner stores or gas stations.

- In the Daily Itineraries, you will notice that directions and landmarks are often noted in very short intervals, sometimes less than a kilometre. Consequently, it would be a good idea to always read two or three of the directions at a time, so that you will not have to stop and read them too frequently. If you want to quicken your pace, you may want to ignore the references to landmarks and concentrate on the directions which indicate turns.

- At the end of the Daily Itineraries section, you will find some connecting tours to Nova Scotia and New Brunswick, via the two ferries that go there. These tours are not as detailed as the others, and are designed to assist those who are cycling to the Island from those provinces. Respectively, they hook up to the Island Daily Itineraries in the middle of Day S at km 11.3, in the middle of Day J at km 96.7, or Day D at km 29.4. These connections are further documented in the Daily Itineraries.

There are nine Recommended Tours of PEI, the Magdalen Islands and Nova Scotia suggested here, varying in length from three-day trips on up to eighteen days. I have provided brief descriptions of each trip, along with the sequence of the lettered Daily Itineraries you should follow from the Daily Itineraries section of this guide. For a more complete description of each tour, you should read the General Route Descriptions of each Daily Itinerary included in the tour you plan to take. The enclosed maps will give you a sense of where each day goes. Unless indicated otherwise, each tour (e.g. Day A, Day L, Day Q) will bring you to the starting point of the next tour day in the sequence. As many of the Daily Itineraries are interconnecting, you can also construct your own tours with a little advance planning. All the tours assume that you will be starting and finishing your tour in Charlottetown. If you are cycling to the Island via one of the two ferries, you should follow one of the connecting routes at the end of the Daily Itineraries section after Day V. These connecting routes hook up with the Daily Itineraries.

Tour 1 (Three Days, Four Nights)
Tour 1 takes you through southeastern Kings County, where you will cycle through inland farm country, and along the southern shore of Kings County. Your overnight stops are in Charlottetown, Brudenell, Murray River, and Charlottetown.

In order, follow Days L, R, and S.

Tour 2 (Five Days, Six Nights)
Tour 2 takes you on a loop throughout Queens County, cycling along both the North and South Shores. Queens County is the most popular county for tourists and affords spectacular views of the beaches. Your overnight stops are in Charlottetown, Brackley Beach, Cavendish Beach, Kensington, Victoria-by-the-Sea, and Charlottetown.

In order, follow Days A, B, C, D, and K.

Tour 3 (Five Days, Six Nights)
Tour 3 crosses inland through Kings County to its eastern shore, goes north to the North Shore of Kings County, and comes back to Charlottetown via the South Shore. Your overnight stops are in Charlottetown, Brudenell, Souris, Brudenell, Murray River, and Charlottetown.

In order, follow Days L, M, Q,* R and S.

Tour 4 (Six Days, Seven Nights)
Tour 4 takes you from Charlottetown through northern Queens County, across the northern shore of Prince County to Tyne Valley, and back along the southern shores of Prince and Queens Counties. Your overnight stops are in Charlottetown, Brackley Beach, Cavendish Beach, Kensington, Tyne Valley, Victoria-by-the-Sea, and Charlottetown.

In order, follow Days A, B, C, E, J, and K.

Tour 5 (Seven Days, Eight Nights)
Tour 5 follows a loop around Queens County, before turning off to cycle through New Brunswick and the northern shore of Nova Scotia. Your overnight stops are in Charlottetown, Brackley Beach, Cavendish Beach, Kensington, Amherst, Tatamagouche, Wood Islands, and Charlottetown.

In order, follow Days A, B, C, D,** T, U, V and S.**

Tour 6 (Eight Days, Nine Nights)
Tour 6 takes you through inland Kings County, visits both shores, and takes you over to the Magdalen Islands for three nights and two days of cycling. Your overnight

---

*Day Q for Tour 3 starts at the Souris, PEI ferry terminal. Follow Day Q's directions starting immediately after the General Route Description for Day Q.

**When you get to Day D on PEI, make sure you turn right at kilometre 29.4, onto Route 1, the connecting route to the New Brunswick ferry. Once in New Brunswick, follow Day T to Amherst. Similarly, after you return to PEI via Day V, follow the connecting route from the Wood Islands ferry terminal to kilometre 11.3 of Day S, where you will follow Day S in to Charlottetown.

stops are in Charlottetown, Brudenell, Souris, Cap-aux-Meules (three nights), Brudenell, Murray River, and Charlottetown.

In order, follow Days L, M, N, O, P, Q, R, and S.

Tour 7 (Ten Days, Eleven Nights)

Tour 7 covers virtually all of the southern and northern shores of Prince and Queens Counties. You will cycle to PEI's northern tip, North Cape. Your overnight stops are in Charlottetown, Brackley Beach, Cavendish Beach, Kensington, Tyne Valley, Alberton, Skinners Pond, West Point, Tyne Valley, Victoria-by-the-Sea, and Charlottetown.

In order, follow days A, B, C, E, F, G, H, I, J, and K.

Tour 8 (Fifteen Days, Sixteen Nights)

Tour 8 covers most of the PEI Daily Itineraries laid out in this guide. You will cycle from one end of PEI to the other, seeing inland farm country, and much of the shoreline. Your overnight stops are in Charlottetown, Brackley Beach, Cavendish Beach, Kensington, Tyne Valley, Alberton, Skinners Pond, West Point, Tyne Valley, Victoria-by-the-Sea, Charlottetown, Brudenell, Souris, Brudenell, Murray River, and Charlottetown.

In order, follow days A, B, C, E, F, G, H, I, J, K, L, M, Q,* R, and S.

Tour 9 (Eighteen Days, Nineteen Nights)

Tour 9 covers most of the PEI and the Magdalen Islands Daily Itineraries laid out in this Guide. You will cycle from one end of PEI to the other, seeing inland farm country, much of the shoreline, and visit most of the Magdalen Islands. A five-hour ferry trip will take you to and from the Magdalen Islands. Your overnight stops will be in Charlottetown, Brackley Beach, Cavendish

---

*Day Q for Tour 8 starts at Souris, PEI ferry terminal. Follow Day Q's directions starting immediately after the General Route Description for Day Q.

Beach, Kensington, Tyne Valley, Victoria-by-the-Sea, Charlottetown, Brudenell, Souris, Cap-aux-Meules (three nights), Brudenell, Murray River, and Charlottetown.

In order, follow Days A, B, C, E, F, G, H, I, J, K, L, M, N, O, P, Q, R, and S.

Day A

START:	Charlottetown
FINISH:	Brackley Beach Area
KM:	45.9

Today's route takes you north from Charlottetown through inland farm country and west along the ocean front beaches of the North Shore. There are local fishing harbours to visit, plenty of easily accessible beaches, and regular stops for water, food, and lunch. Accommodations should be selected in the Covehead, Stanhope, Brackley, and Tracadie sections of the Visitors Guide. Campgrounds, hotels, and farm tourist homes are available.

Directions

Find your way to the corner of Grafton and University, the centre of downtown Charlottetown. Once there, follow these directions carefully until you leave the modest hubbub of Charlottetown traffic. As you face the war memorial in front of Province House, go left (east) down Grafton Street until you reach Edward Street. Turn left onto Edward Street at the Ultramar gas station.

0.8 km

Take your first right onto Kent Street, which turns into Kensington Avenue as you cross the railroad tracks.

0.9 km

Stay on Kensington Avenue until it ends at Riverside Drive. Turn left onto Riverside Drive.

3.7 km

Stay on Riverside Drive, going straight through the lights, until it ends at a stop sign. At the stop sign, turn right onto Route 15, also known as Brackley Point Road.

5.6 km

Stay on Route 15, passing the airport on your right, until you reach Route 221, known as Union Road. Turn right onto Union Road (221). You'll see Dalzell Auto Body on your left, just before the turn on your right. You have now left the busy Charlottetown traffic behind. Until you reach Tracadie harbour, you will be cycling through quiet, pastoral Prince Edward Island. You will see a lot of potato farms on your way to the North Shore.

8.0 km

Continue on Union Road until you see a sign for Route 220. Travel for 0.5 of a km *after* the sign, turn right onto Route 220. For a short while, it is a well-maintained dirt road. Watch your mileage to make sure you don't miss this turn.

12.7 km

Stay on Route 220, crossing Route 25, until 220 ends. Turn right onto Route 6.

22.6 km

Stay on Route 6 until you see the Grand Tracadie Elementary School on your left. Take a sharp left onto the paved road.

23.6 km

Stay on the paved road until you reach Tracadie harbour, a good place to have lunch, to get to know a typical Island lobster fishing harbour, and to enjoy the dune-enclosed harbour. The ocean is particulary warm here, owing to the shallow water surrounding the beach. Tracadie is a favourite hideaway for Islanders.

26.0 km

Return the way you have come, back towards the Grand Tracadie Elementary School. Turn right onto Route 6 at the school.

28.4 km

Go straight on Route 6 until you see the National Park gates/toll booth in front of you. Go straight through the National Park gates onto the National Park road. You have now left Route 6, which turned off just before the gates.

30.9 km

For the next 10 km you will be cycling along the North Shore, which will be on your right. By crossing the rolling dunes, you can access the beach just about anywhere to take a swim in surprisingly warm water. On your left, you will notice a large, turn-of-the-century wood mansion on Dalvay Pond. This is the Dalvay by the Sea Hotel, where some of the *Anne of Geen Gables* movie was filmed. It is worth a visit. Shortly after the Dalvay Hotel, on your left, is a National Park Nature Walk, with signs detailing the ecology and life cycle of the surrounding environment. Stop in for a short stroll and a break.

33.6 km

Continue on the National Park road towards Covehead harbour. If you have selected an accommodation for tonight, it is probably in this general area or just after you leave the National Park down Route 15. Just before Covehead harbour, you will see a turnoff for Stanhope-by-the-Sea Hotel, a resort hotel offering complete boating and water skiing facilities. It's a short detour if you're interested: just follow the Bayshore Road to your left onto Route 25. When you get to Covehead harbour, you will see an ocean front lighthouse on your right. (Good place for a lighthouse, when you think about it.) Turn left to go into Covehead harbour, where you can buy fresh lobster, lobster burgers, and deep fried clams, or go deep-sea fishing for cod and mackerel with a number of different outfits. Deep-sea fishing costs around twelve dollars per person for three hours. The skippers are generally very warm, good-humoured and helpful. After visiting Covehead harbour, go back the way you came and turn left onto the National Park road.

38.5 km

Cross the bridge and continue on until you see another set of National Park gates/toll booths to your left. Turn left to go through them and leave the National Park. You are now on the northern end of Route 15.

43.3 km

Go straight down Route 15 toward Route 6. Your first left will take you into Shaw's Hotel, a nineteenth-century family-run resort hotel. Shaw's dining room overlooks Covehead harbour and is a good spot for a lobster supper tonight. Further down Route 15, you will see the Dunes Studio and Gallery, a great place for local pottery and crafts. At the corner of Routes 15 and 6 is a Visitor Information Centre on your left and an Irving gas station on your right. Along this short stretch you will see a few grocery stores, lunch bars, and restaurants. If you are having trouble finding your accommodations, the staff at the Visitor Information Centre should be able to help you.

45.9 km.

Day B

START: Brackley Beach Area
FINISH: Cavendish Area
KM: 43.3

Today's route takes you on or near the North Shore following Route 6, the National Park road, and some smaller routes. You will see Green Gables house, historical villages and fishing harbours, and Cavendish Beach, and you will cycle along the red-cliffed Cavendish Capes, overlooking the ocean. While the distances are short today, there is a lot to see. Motels, farm tourist homes, and campgrounds are available. Select accommodations from the Cavendish and Stanley Bridge sections of the Visitors Guide.

Directions

As you face south on Route 15 at the corner of Route 6, turn right onto Route 6 and stay on it. The Visitor Information Centre is on your left, the Irving gas station is to your right. When you get to Oyster Bed Bridge, you will see the Oyster Bed Bridge General Store and gas station on your left. Turn right to stay on Route 6.

3.8 km

As you cross a small bridge, you will see Café St. Jean on your left (good place for lunch) and Gaudreau's Fine Woodworking on your right (stop in for a demonstration and to browse for Island crafts). Turn right immediately after the bridge onto Route 242, the road in front of Gaudreau's Fine Woodworking.

6.2 km

Follow Route 242 (which is a loop running along the ocean) back to Route 6. When you arrive at Route 6, you will see Winter Creek Farm in front of you and Gallant Food Market to your right. Turn right onto Route 6.

11.9 km

Once on Route 6, take your next quick right onto Route 243. On Route 243 you will see the Stella Maris Credit Union to your left.

12.1 km

As you arrive in Rustico, you will see St. Augustin Church in front of you, worth a visit, and the Rustico Farmer's Bank Museum to your right. The Farmer's Bank is Canada's first credit union. Admission to the museum, which documents much of Rustico's history, is one dollar.

13.1 km

As you face St. Augustin Church, go to your left, following Route 243 out of Rustico. When you get to a fork in the road, take a hard left onto a dirt road.

15.1 km

When you see the Summer Haven sign at the end of the dirt road, turn left to stay on Route 243.

16.0 km

At the end of Route 243, you will come back to Route 6. Turn right onto Route 6.

18.4 km

Along Route 6, you will cross a small bridge, with the fishing harbour on your right, where rows of white buoys indicate mussel farming. When you get to North Rustico, you will see Fisherman's Wharf Lobster Suppers on your right, as well as grocery stores and a gas station. Turn right immediately after Fisherman's Wharf Lobster Suppers. You are headed towards North Rustico Harbour.

23.4 km

At the end of the road, stop at North Rustico Harbour. Visit the lighthouse, the Court Brothers, the Seagull's Nest Craft Shop or go deep-sea fishing. The Seagull's Nest offers hot air balloon rides.

25.1 km

Return the way you came, back towards North Rustico and Fisherman's Wharf Lobster Suppers. Turn right onto Churchill Avenue, which is just before the post office. You are on your way to the National Park road and the Cavendish Capes.

26.8 km

Turn left at the National Park gates and onto the National Park road.

28.0 km

Stop at the sign for Orby Head on your right, and turn onto the dirt drive. You will come to hundred-foot, time-sculpted red cliffs overlooking the ocean. Orby Head is one of the highest points on the North Shore, so you will be able to look east and west at miles of shoreline. Spectacular sight, good place for lunch or a snack. Your route continues straight on the National Park road.

32.1 km

Turn left at the Green Gables sign (the setting of Lucy Maud Montgomery's *Anne of Green Gables*), and go through the National Park gates.

35.8 km

Continue straight for 1.1 km until you reach Route 6. Turn right onto Route 6 at the lights. You will see the Wax Museum on your left and the Anne Shirley Motel in front of you.

36.9 km

Turn left at the Green Gables sign at the bottom of the hill, just after the golf cart cross-walk.

37.1 km

Follow this entrance drive for 0.4 km, until you reach Green Gables House. You might like to stop and visit Prince Edward Island's most famous nineteenth-century home, the setting of *Anne of Green Gables*. Tours are free, quick, and give you a real feel for Island history.

37.5 km

Retrace your steps back to the National Park gates you just left. Go back down the drive, turn right onto Route 6, left at the Wax Museum, left at the National Park gates, and back onto the National Park road.

39.2 km

Continue straight in the same direction (west) until you reach Cavendish Beach, one of the Island's most beautiful and popular beaches. Snack bar and restrooms are available.

40.4 km

Continue on the National Park road and through the gates until you get to Route 6. In front of you, to your right, are the Cavendish Tourist Mart, Thirsty's Bar and Restaurant, and the Sunset Campgrounds. There are a lot of campgrounds and accommodations in this area, so this is a good time to consult your Visitors Guide, if you have not already done so. The Cavendish Tourist Mart has excellent ice cream, Island clothing, a book store, and groceries. You are now at the corner of the National Park road and Route 6. Tomorrow you will go right (west) on Route 6.

Your accommodations should be somewhere in this area. A personal favourite is Lyndon Cove Farm Tourist Home on Route 238 off Route 6, near Stanley Bridge. It is listed in the Visitors Guide under Stanley Bridge. Follow your Visitors Guide carefully to get there. Day C's directions take you past the turnoff for Route 238.

If you want to enjoy Island summer night life, tonight is the night to do it, on the Cavendish Strip (Thirsty's, Cavendish Arms Pub, or Gilligan's Landing, all on Route 6 between Cavendish and Stanley Bridge).

43.3 km

Day C

START: Cavendish Area
FINISH: Kensington
KM: 44.1

Today's route takes you west through northwestern Queens County, northeastern Prince County, and south to Kensington. You will be travelling along Routes 6, 20, and 104. You will see the birthplace of Lucy Maud Montgomery, local potters and crafts in New London, pass through the valley harbour of French River, and visit Malpeque Bay, the home of the world famous Malpeque oysters. Hotels and farm tourist homes are available. The nearest campground is Rayner's Park at Weber Cove in Lower New Annan, near the intersection of Routes 120 and 106. Accommodations should be selected in the Kensington section of the Visitors Guide. Rayner's Park is listed in the camping section under Summerside.

Directions

Start at the corner of Route 6 and the National Park road, the end of Day B. Turn right (west) onto Route 6 and go straight until you reach a four-road intersection (the junction of Routes 224, 254, and 6), where you will see a craft store, a Shell station and the Stanley Bridge Church. On the way, you will pass Gilligan's Landing, and if you're into jet skiing, or would like to be, this is the place to do it. At the intersection, turn right to stay on Route 6.

3.8 km

Still on Route 6, you will see New London Lions Lobster Suppers on your left, one of the Island's best lobster suppers. Good place to stop and have steamed clams, mussels, or a lobster burger. Continue on Route 6 towards New London.

6.3 km

When you get to New London, you will probably want to take a break. (That was some hill, wasn't it?) In New London, you'll see the Village Pottery Store on your right, an Irving gas station on the corner and, just around the corner, Lucy Maud Montgomery's birthplace, which is also a small museum of Island history. Turn right at the gas station onto Route 20. You are headed towards French River.

8.3 km

Arriving in French River, you would be wise to buy any snacks or supplies you may need, as you are now heading into a less-developed part of the Island. You will see the Jollimore Grocery Store on your right. French River's history goes back to the 1700s, when American cargo ships were blown in by storms. Your route continues straight.

15.1 km

Coming up on your right, you will see the turnoff for the Penderosa Beach Cottages and Campground. They offer windsurfing and beach facilities. Good for an afternoon break. Today's route continues straight.

24.4 km

When you reach the next Irving station and the Princetown Church on your right, turn left to stay on Route 20. You are in Malpeque, named for the famous oysters in nearby Malpeque Bay. The flower gardens in Malpeque feature 400 varieties of dahlia. The Princetown Art Gallery is on your right, and definitely worth a visit. In front of you is one of the few bicycle shops you will see outside Charlottetown.

29.6 km

Coming up on your right, you will see the Malpeque View Corner Store. Turn right onto Route 104. This route is a short loop off Route 20, which will take you through Indian River and past an access road to Malpeque Bay.

31.5 km

Your next landmark is a large white and red wooden church, St. Mary's, designed in the 1880s by William Critchlow Harris. Harris designed twenty churches on Prince Edward Island, all in the Gothic style. Sixteen remain today.

38.6 km

If you are headed towards Rayner's Park Campground, you will want to turn off onto Route 106 after Indian River (follow your Visitors Map to Lower New Annan). Otherwise, you will keep going straight on Route 104 until you rejoin Route 20, by turning right onto it.

39.3 km

You are now headed towards Kensington. When you reach the traffic lights (Victoria Street and Route 20), you will be in the centre of Kensington, where you should find your accommodations for tonight. Kensington is one of the Island's larger towns, so it is a good place to stock up on harder to get supplies, particularly if you are heading west, where the Island is less-populated. This is the end of Day C, and the starting point for Day D, and Day E.

44.1 km

Day D

START:	Kensington
FINISH:	Victoria-by-the-Sea
KM:	47.5

Today's route takes you south from Kensington on Routes 109, 8, 110, 112, and 10 to the South Shore harbour town of Victoria. You will be cycling through south-eastern Prince County, which is quite quiet and untravelled and consists mostly of long stretches of farmland. One of the only corner stores/lunch bars you will see along the way is The Village Store in Bedeque (on Route 112), so if you are not carrying your lunch with you, this should be your lunch stop. Hotels, farm tourist homes and campgrounds are available. Hotels and farm tourist homes should be selected from the Victoria section of the Visitors Guide. Campgrounds available are Redcliffe Downs Travel Park, listed under Hampton in the Visitors Guide, on the Trans Canada Highway, four km past Victoria; and Cumberland Cove Campground, listed under Augustine Cove in the Visitors Guide, on Route 10, twelve km before you arrive in Victoria. Accommodations in Victoria are almost always full in the summer, so be sure to book in advance.

Directions
Start at the corner of Route 20 and Victoria Street, facing in the same direction you were when you finished Day C (with the post office in front of you to your right). Turn

right onto Victoria Street and then take your first quick left onto Kelvin Road, which is Route 109.

0.1 km

Turn right onto Route 107.

2.7 km

Take your first left back onto Route 109.

3.1 km

Continue on Route 109 until its end at Route 8, which is not marked. Turn right onto Route 8. You will see the Freetown Birch Grove Hall on your left.

7.6 km

On Route 8, to your left you will see a Texaco station, one of your last stops for a while to get water and snacks. You are in the area of Freetown. Continue on Route 8.

7.9 km

This next turn onto Route 110 is very easy to miss as there are *no* road signs whatsoever. It is the next paved left after the Texaco station you just passed. On your right in the distance you will see the Lower Freetown School; at the turn on your left you will see a green barn and a white house. Turn left onto Route 110.

11.3 km

Stay on Route 110 until you cross a small bridge, a good place to spot blue herons, and climb the short hill. You will see signs in front of you indicating Bedeque and Middleton. You are going to Bedeque, so turn right to get onto Route 10.

13.9 km

Go straight on Route 10, crossing the major highway 1A, passing Callbeck's Hardware Store and IGA on your right, until you reach a good spot for lunch, the Bedeque Village Store, which is on your right. You are now in Bedeque. After lunch, turn left onto Route 112.

18.3 km

Stay on Route 112 until you reach the flashing lights and Route 10. Turn right onto Route 10.

22.5 km

On your right on Route 10, you will see St. Peters Church. If you're lucky, the caretaker, Arnold, will be there. He has been working at this church for over sixty years and will be eager to tell you its history. He has come to know cyclists and keeps an eye out for their arrival.

25.0 km

Keep going straight on Route 10, crossing the major Route 1, where you can stop for water and snacks at the ESSO station on your right. If you are going to the New Brunswick ferry, turn right onto Route 1. Otherwise, today's route continues straight.

29.4 km

Still on Route 10, you may want to stop at the ice boat fishing monument, which will be on your left. This is an exhibit detailing the first ferry service to the Island, which was run in a small wooden boat equipped with runners for the purpose of traversing ice flows.

31.1 km

Continue on Route 10 until you reach a fork in the road (just after a steep decline and the small bridge, which was built by the Dutch settlers as a dam for flooding farmland). You are now in Tryon. Turn right at the fork in the road onto Route 116.

41.1 km

On your left you will see the Tryon River Studio Gallery, the studio of Island etcher Steve Clements. Cyclists have been stopping by the gallery for years, and Steve will offer you a demonstration of the etching process. It is well worth the half-hour, if not for any interest you have in the etching process then for Steve's considerable knowledge about the history of the Tryon area.

41.7 km

Continue on Route 116, which will turn into a dirt road for a kilometre and a half. Stay left until you reach the end of Route 116, where you will be facing a church. You are now in Victoria-by-the-Sea. Turn right.

47.1 km

Turn left at the Victoria Fire Hall, which is on your right. You are now on Main Street, where you will see the Victoria Village Inn and the Victoria Playhouse. Just around the corner (everything is just around the corner in Victoria) are the Orient Hotel, Sea Shed Crafts, the Victoria Playhouse (top quality summer theatre run by cycling enthusiast Erskine Smith), and the Island Chocolate Factory. This is the end of Day D. Your accommodations should be somewhere nearby.

47.5 km

Day E

START:	Kensington
FINISH:	Tyne Valley
KM:	81.8 km

Today's route takes you south, west and north through the eastern end of Prince County via Routes 109, 107, 11, 128, 132, and 178. You will pass through the Island's second largest community—Summerside, visit the South and North Shores, experience traditional French Acadian culture in the Evangeline region, see the Notre Dame du Mont Carmel Cathedral, cycle for miles along ocean front red cliffs, and arrive in Tyne Valley, the home of the summer oyster shucking contest. Today's route is quite long, so a shortcut has been suggested at km 26.8. You will see many of the oldest farmhouses and communities today, as the Evangeline region is one of the earliest French settlements on the Island. Accommodations should be selected in the Tyne Valley section of the

Visitors Guide. (There are only two inns, so book early!) The only campground available is Green Park Provincial Park in Port Hill on Route 12, four km north of Tyne Valley.

Directions

Start at the corner of Route 20 and Victoria Street, facing in the same direction you were when you finished Day C. Turn right onto Victoria Street, and then take your first quick left onto Kelvin Road (Route 109).

0.1 km

At the end of Route 109, turn right onto Route 107.

3.4 km

Turn right onto Route 1A at the end of Route 107. You'll see a bridge at the turnoff.

12.4 km

On your left, you will see a Visitor Information Centre.

12.6 km

At the ESSO station you will see a sign indicating Summerside. Here you will turn left onto Water Street, Route 11. Stay straight on Water Street all the way through Summerside.

13.7 km

Keep an eye out for the Eptek Centre on your left, your cue to bear right off Route 11 to stay on Water Street. When you get to Bayview Avenue, you will see St. Eleanor's Dairy Bar and Take-Out, where you will turn left back onto Route 11.

19.9 km

If you want to bypass the South Shore and shorten today's route, this is the place to do it, at Route 12, where you will see a sign for Misgouche. If you are taking the shortcut, turn right onto Route 12, which you can follow all the way to Tyne Valley. The main route continues straight on Route 11.

26.8 km

Just after the small United Church on your left is one of the Island's lesser-known Provincial Parks—Union Corner Park, well worth the visit—with one of those beaches where you can walk out into the ocean for a great distance before the water is over your head. Your route continues straight on Route 11.

38.7 km

On your left is one of the oldest churches on the Island. Eglise Notre Dame du Carmel, beautiful in its own right, accords a stunning view of the South Shore cliffs. Continue on Route 11.

42.5 km

You are now passing through the first Acadian village, where you may want to stop and have a typical Acadian lunch at the restored traditional community on your right.

43.7 km

On your left is the Cape Egmont wharf, another quiet spot on the South Shore with a great view.

48.2 km

Another wharf! This one is named after the Acadian Abram-Village you will soon be passing through

55.3 km

The next turn is easy to miss. When you arrive in Abram-Village, you will see a Texaco station on your left, at the intersection of Routes 124 and 11. Turn left to stay on Route 11.

58.2 km

Coming up is a small corner store, the last one you will see for a while, so stock up if you need to.

58.6 km

On your right is the Eglise St. Philipe-St. Jacques, another historic French Catholic Church, which you may want to visit.

61.5 km

When you get to St. Chrysostome, stay straight to turn off Route 11 and onto Route 128 north towards Tyne Valley.

67.5 km

At the end of Route 128, turn left onto Route 2.

73.7 km

Take your first quick right onto Route 132.

74.5 km

Just after you get to the railroad tracks, turn left onto Route 178, the last leg to Tyne Valley.

77.1 km

Turn left at the stop sign and stop at the post office on your left. You're here! If you're staying in one of the inns, you will be able to see them both from here. Before you put your feet up for the night, you may want to stop in at Tyne Valley's famous Tea Room and Craft Shop or have some freshly shucked raw oysters, Tyne Valley's specialty. You have cycled a long way today (unless you took the shortcut), so enjoy your evening and the gentle, relaxing atmosphere of Tyne Valley.

81.8 km

Day F

START:	Tyne Valley
FINISH:	Alberton
KM:	43.7 km

Today's route takes you northwest towards Alberton via Routes 12, and 2, then back on 12. You will cycle over Cascumpec Bay, have an option to visit the Indian Reserve on Lennox Island with its view of Bird Island, and pass by the long, thin islands off the North Shore. Accommodations should be selected from the Alberton section of the Visitors Guide. There is one farm tourist home, one bed and breakfast, and one motel. The nearest campground is Jacques Cartier Provincial Park, 5 km east of Alberton, off Route 12, near the Kildare Capes.

Directions
Starting at the end point of Day E, turn right at the post office, then take a left at MacNeil's Corner Store onto Route 12 heading northwest. On your right is the Tyne Valley Tea Room.

0.1 km

Stay on Route 12 until you see the turnoff for Lennox Island, where you will see Lennox Mic Mac crafts. This is an *optional* turnoff. Route 163 will be on your right. Lennox Island is 4.8 km along the turnoff. Your route continues straight on Route 12.

5.9 km

Heading in the same direction on Route 12, you will see a grocery store/ESSO station. It is the only store for the next eleven km.

9.9 km

The Freeland Presbyterian Church, worth a visit and a good spot for a rest, is your cue to turn left to stay on Route 12.

11.5 km

Just after St. Peter's Church, at St. Brigid's Catholic Cemetery on your right, turn left to cross a small river and stay on Route 12.

15.9 km

At the Irving gas station/corner store in Portage, turn right onto Route 2. You will cycle on this busy route for 2.7 km.

21.2 km

Turn right, back onto Route 12, towards Alberton.

23.9 km

Coming up on your right you will see a corner store/gas station. Just past the corner store is Mill River, a bridge and a public beach with some of the warmest water on the Island. Continue straight on Route 12.

37.7 km

At the junction of Routes 12 and 150, turn right to stay on Route 12. At this corner, you will see a sign for cooked lobster, a good place to pick up some dinner if you're camping out at the Jacques Cartier Provincial Park.

42.4 km

The flashing lights indicate your arrival in Alberton. You will see the Westerner Motel at the corner. Alberton is a good place to buy any supplies you need for your bicycle as there is a modestly equipped sport store. You will also find a pharmacy, and hardware and grocery stores.

43.7 km

Day G

START:	Alberton
FINISH:	Skinners Pond
KM:	65.6

Today's route takes you in a half-loop around the north-western tip of the Island, along Routes 12 and 14. You will be cycling along stark, cliffed shoreline, towards the Atlantic Wind Test site, the North Cape Lighthouse (a beautiful spot for lunch, seventy-five feet above a panoramic view of the ocean), and south towards the small fishing village and home of Stompin' Tom Connors, Skinners Pond. Today's route is *very* lightly populated, with few corner stores, so you would be wise to have plenty of water and food with you. Accommodations can be found in the Skinners Pond section of the Visitors Guide, with two farm tourist homes available.

The only campground available is the Harbour Lights Trailer Park just outside Skinners Pond on Route 14.

Directions
Start from the flashing lights where you ended Day F. Go straight through the flashing lights onto Route 12, past the church. Make sure you have lots of snacks and food, because nothing *except* water will be available for the next 32.5 km. During this part of the route, you will have spectacular views of old churches, shoreline, and sparse farm country. Follow Route 12 until you see the Atlantic Wind Test site.

32.5 km

Continue straight on Route 12 until you get to the North Cape Lighthouse, the northernmost point of the Island. These cliffs have dirt roads which continue around their perimeter and are a nice place to go for a lunchtime stroll.

32.9 km

Turn around and retrace your route back onto Route 12, and follow these directions *very* carefully, following your Visitors Map so as not to miss a poorly marked turn-off to Christopher Cross, Nail Pond, and Skinners Pond. Just after the sign to Christopher Cross, you will see two roads, one paved and one dirt. Turn right onto the paved road; this is Route 14.

54.4 km

Continue straight on Route 14 until you reach a stop sign, where you will have a choice of going left or right. Go right to stay on Route 14.

56.1 km

Continue on Route 14 until you reach the Skinners Pond harbour sign. Turn right towards the Skinners Pond harbour.

65.6 km

Go straight down to the fishing harbour, one of the Island's oldest. Perry's Take-Out sells fresh seafood, lobster burgers and oysters. This is the end of Day G. Your accommodations should be nearby. The Harbour Lights Trailer Park is two km south on Route 14.

65.6 km

Day H

Start: Skinners Pond
Finish: West Point
Km: 50.7

Today's route takes you south along Route 14, almost entirely ocean front cliffs, toward West Point. You will see the old Acadian village of Miminegash, see plenty of beach front, get a chance to go seal watching, and see some more of the historic churches and cemeteries of the Island. There are more gas stations and corner stores than there were in Days F and G, so you needn't be as concerned about stocking up on supplies before you set out. Accommodations should be selected from the West Point section of the Visitors Guide, with a bed and breakfast and lighthouse accommodations available. The West Point Lighthouse offers unique luxury accommodations in their tower room, which includes a spectacular view and whirlpool bath, with champagne and breakfast included to round out a unique experience. A seafood restaurant is located on the premises. The only campground available is the Cedar Dunes Provincial Park, 0.4 km from West Point harbour on Route 14.

Directions
Start at Day G's end point, at Skinners Pond. Go back out to Route 14 and turn right.

0.6 km

As you cycle through Miminegash, you will see an optional turnoff to the Miminegash harbour on your right at the Irving station. Your route continues straight on Route 14.

14.0 km

Jennie's Place and Take-Out at the Irving station is a good place for a snack and a break.

30.0 km

Howard's Cove is another spot to enjoy fresh seafood while taking in an expansive view of the ocean. Just past Howard's Cove is a right turnoff to Seal Point, so named because it is a good spot to go seal watching. Your route continues straight.

34.8 km

As you approach West Point, keep an eye out for the West Point harbour sign, after which you will turn right to go down to West Point, an historic lighthouse location, and one of the Island's larger fishing harbours. Turn right.

49.7 km

As you arrive in West Point harbour, you will see Fred's Grocery Store, the only grocery store in the neighbourhood. It is *only* open in the afternoon, so make sure to buy tomorrow's supplies today.

50.3 km

The West Point Lighthouse is located in Cedar Dunes Provincial Park, which is 0.4 km to your left. This is the end of Day H.

50.7 km

Day I

START: West Point
FINISH: Tyne Valley
KM: 48.6

Today's route takes you north and east back to Tyne Valley, also the overnight stop at the end of Day E. You will be cycling mostly through inland farm country, and during the first half of the day you will once again be in a less-populated area of the Island, so it's a good idea to have all the necessary supplies. Accommodations should be selected in the Tyne Valley section of the Visitors Guide. (There are only two inns, so book early!) The only campground available is Green Park Provincial Park in Port Hill on Route 12, 4 km north of Tyne Valley.

Directions:
Starting at the West Point harbour, the end point of Day H, go back up to Route 14 and turn right onto it.

0.7 km

When you see a small dam near the road, turn right to stay on Route 14. If you are there during the spawning season, you will see salmon leaping over the dam.

6.0 km

When you reach a fork in the road, you will see a sign indicating the Lady Slipper Drive. Turn right to stay on Route 14.

17.9 km

When you reach the end of Route 14, turn right onto Route 2, the main highway, where you will see an ESSO station. Route 2 is quite busy, as it is one of the Island's main highways, so cycle with caution.

22.1 km

At the *second* turnoff to Route 12, turn left onto Route 12. You are in Portage and headed towards Tyne Valley. There is an Irving station and grocery store on the corner.

27.4 km

At St. Brigid's Catholic Cemetery, turn right to stay on Route 12.

32.7 km

At Freeland Presbyterian Church, turn right to stay on Route 12.

37.1 km

At the Lennox Mic Mac Craft Store, you will have an optional turn to visit Lennox Island, an historic Mic Mac Indian reserve, which affords a view of migrating birds on Bird Island. Your route continues straight on Route 12.

42.7 km

As you enter Tyne Valley, you will see the Tyne Valley Tea Room on your left and MacNeil's Grocery on your right. Turn right at MacNeil's and stop at the post office. If you're staying in one of the inns, you'll be able to see them both from here. Before you put your feet up for the night, you may want to stop in at Tyne Valley's famous Tea Room and Craft Shop or have some freshly shucked raw oysters, Tyne Valley's specialty. This is the end of Day I.

48.6 km

Day J

Start:	Tyne Valley
Finish:	Victoria
Km:	114.8

Today's route takes you back along the route you cycled during the second half of Day E, unless you took the shortcut along Route 12, which you can also take today.

The route is the longest in this guide, at least eight hours of cycling, so it would be wise to leave Tyne Valley early in the morning. The shortcut via Route 12 leaves east from Tyne Valley and hugs Malpeque Bay down to Misgouche, where you can join up with the rest of the longer route mapped out for today on Route 11 (km 54.2 in today's itinerary). The longer route for today takes you south and east, following Routes 178, 132, 2, 128, 11, 1A, 107, 110, and 10 to Victoria.

You will cycle through the Région Evangeline and along shoreline through most of the first half of the day, and inland, hilly farm country during the second half of the day. As you can probably tell, there are a lot of turns and routes today, many of them poorly marked, so pay close attention to these directions. Hotels, farm tourist homes, and campgrounds are available. Hotels and farm tourist homes should be selected from the Victoria section of the Visitors Guide. Campgrounds available are Redcliffe Downs Travel Park, listed under Hampton in the Visitors Guide, on the Trans Canada Highway, four km past Victoria; and Cumberland Cove Campground, listed under Augustine Cove in the Visitors Guide, on Route 10, twelve km before you arrive in Victoria. A favourite is the Orient Hotel, an historical hotel dating to the turn of the century and recently restored by owners Lee Jollife and Darrel Tschirhart. Victoria accommodations are almost always full in the summer, so be sure to book in advance.

Directions
Starting at the end point of Day I, take a left at the post office towards Route 178. It is not marked, so ensure you get on the right road heading out of town. Take a right at the stop sign to get onto Route 178.

0.1 km

Continue down Route 178 to Route 132, and the railroad tracks crossing it. Turn right onto Route 132.

4.7 km

At the end of Route 132, turn left onto Route 2.

7.3 km

Take your first quick right onto Route 128.

8.1 km

At the end of Route 128, at St. Chrysostome, turn left onto Route 11.

14.3 km

The Eglise St. Philipe-St. Jacques is another historic Acadian church you may want to visit.

20.3 km

As you get to the Texaco station, at the intersection of Routes 124 and 11 (you are on Route 11), turn right to stay on Route 11. You are now in Abram-Village.

23.6 km

The Abram-Village wharf is on your right.

26.5 km

The Cap Egmont wharf is on your right. It has a great view of the South Shore.

33.6 km

One of the oldest churches on the Island, the Eglise Notre Dame du Carmel, is beautiful in its own right, and affords a stunning view of the South Shore cliffs.

39.3 km

One of the Island's lesser-known Provincial Parks is Union Corner Provincial Park on your right, and well worth the visit. The ocean is quite shallow for about a mile and almost always has active surf. Your route continues straight.

42.1 km

When you see the sign for Miscouche, keep right to stay on Route 11. If you have taken the Route 12 shortcut, this is where you will join up today's route on your way to Victoria.

54.2 km

As you come in to the outskirts of St. Eleanors, Route 11 will have the street name Bayview Avenue. At St. Eleanors Dairy Bar and Take-Out, turn right onto Water Street.

60.1 km

After you cycle on Water Street through Summerside you will see an ESSO station at Route 1A. Turn right onto Route 1A.

66.3 km

On your right you will see a Visitors Information Centre.

67.4 km

Just before the bridge turn left onto Route 107.

67.6 km

At the sign indicating Lower Freetown, turn right onto Route 110.

73.8 km

When you arrive at the Lower Freetown School, turn right at the yield sign, and then take your first quick left to stay on Route 110.

78.6 km

Stay on Route 110 until you cross a small bridge (a good place to spot blue herons) and climb the short hill. You will see signs that say Bedeque and Middleton. You are going to Bedeque, so turn right to get onto Route 10.

81.2 km

Go straight on Route 10, crossing the major highway 1A, passing Callbeck's Hardware Store and IGA on your right, until you reach Bedeque and a good spot for lunch, the Bedeque Village Store, also on your right. After lunch, turn left onto Route 112.

85.6 km

Stay on Route 112 until you reach the flashing lights and Route 10. Turn right.

89.8 km

On your right on Route 10 you will see St. Peter's Church. If you're lucky, the caretaker, Arnold, will be there. He has been working at this church for over 60 years and will be eager to tell you its history. He has come to know cyclists and keeps an eye out for their arrival.

92.3 km

Keep going straight on Route 10, crossing the major Highway 1, where you can stop for water and snacks at the ESSO station on your right.

96.7 km

Still on Route 10, you may want to stop at the ice boat fishing monument on your right. This is an exhibit detailing the first ferry service to the Island, which was run in a small wooden boat equipped with runners to traverse ice flows.

98.4 km

Continue on Route 10 until you reach a fork in the road just after a steep decline and a small bridge built by the first Dutch settlers as a dam for flooding farmland. You are now in Tryon. Turn right at the fork in the road onto Route 116.

108.4 km

On your left you will see the Tryon River Studio Gallery, the studio of Island etcher Steve Clements. Cyclists have been stopping by the gallery for years, and Steve will offer you a demonstration of the etching process. It is well worth the half-hour, if not for any interest you have in the etching process then for Steve's considerable knowledge about the history of the Tryon area.

109.0 km

Continue on Route 116, which will turn into a dirt road for a kilometre and a half. Stay left until you reach the end of Route 116, where you will be facing a church. You are now in Victoria-by-the-Sea. Turn right.

114.4 km

Turn left at the Victoria Fire Hall, which is on your right. You are now on Main Street, where you will see the Victoria Village Inn and the Victoria Tea Room. Just around the corner (everything is just around the corner in Victoria) are the Orient Hotel, Sea Shed Crafts, the Victoria Playhouse (top quality summer theatre), and the Island Chocolate Factory. This is the end of Day J. The three main accommodations in Victoria are all within a block. Three-hour schooner cruises are available at the Victoria wharf, with departures in the morning and afternoon.

114.8 km

Day K

START: Victoria-by-the-Sea
FINISH: Charlottetown
KM: 41.2

Today's route takes you east and north along Routes 1, 19, 248, and back on Route 1 to Charlottetown. You will cycle along the South Shore of Queens County and have ample opportunity to swim in the warm waters of the South Shore. The red, sandy beaches have extreme high and low tides, particularly around Rice Point where, at low tide, you can walk out for about a kilometre to the shallow waters. You will also have a view of St. Peters Island, where Islanders will tell you a burning ghost ship can often be seen at night, an enduring Island legend.

Just past Canoe Cove, you will have the option to lengthen your route by cycling around Rocky Point to visit the archaeological excavations of the first British and French forts on the Island: Fort Amherst and Port la Joie. The only snack bar along the way is the Shore Store at km 13.5, where you can buy snacks and groceries. Accommodations should be selected from the

Charlottetown section of the Visitors Guide. The two luxury hotels in Charlottetown are the Charlottetown and the CP. A favourite small inn is the Duchess of Kent, with inexpensive, clean, beautifully antique-furnished rooms. It is almost always full, so be sure to book ahead. The nearest campground to Charlottetown is the Southport Trailer Park. To get there, follow Grafton Street to the Hillsborough Bridge, cross the bridge and turn right on Stratford Road.

Directions

Start at the corner of Main and Water Streets, facing the Victoria wharf. Go left on Water Street, towards the lighthouse.

0.0 km

Turn right at the lighthouse.

0.1 km

You will cross a small bridge and see a Provincial Park on your right. At the end of the road, turn left at the yield sign.

1.8 km

The stop sign marks the intersection of Route 1. Turn right onto Route 1.

3.0 km

You are cycling on Route 1 for the next four km. Route 1 is the Trans Canada Highway, so be sure to be cautious and cycle well over on the shoulder. When you see the DeSable Motel on your right and/or the sign to Route 19, turn right onto Route 19.

7.0 km

For the next 25 km you will be cycling along shoreline, where you may want to visit the warm waters of the South Shore. On your left you will see a small corner store, Darren's.

10.9 km

On your right is the Shore Store, the only snack bar you will see on today's route until you get to the outskirts of Charlottetown.

13.5 km

If you want to take a short detour to a small beach and Provincial Park, keep an eye out on your right for the sign to the Keir Presbyterian Camp. To get to the park, turn right and stay right on the dirt road until you see the park. Your route continues straight on Route 19.

18.1 km

The next turn is easy to miss. On your left you will see the yellow Canoe Cove School. Turn right just opposite it to stay on Route 19 and the Blue Heron Drive.

18.6 km

When you come to the fork in the road, follow the sign to New Dominion, turning left. (To your right is an optional detour to Fort Amherst and Port la Joie. If you take this detour you will rejoin the main route at km 27.9.) Turn left to continue on today's route.

26.7 km

When you get to the stop sign, turn left, following the sign to New Dominion. (The detour to Fort Amherst/Port la Joie joins up here. If you took the detour, you continue straight towards New Dominion.) You are now on the final leg of Route 19, which can be busy and has no shoulder, so be cautious.

27.9 km

At the fork in the road, stay right, following the sign to Cornwall.

29.1 km

Route 19 ends at the intersection of Route 1, where you will see the Blue Horizon Motel on your right. Go right onto Route 1 and then, about twenty yards later, your first quick right again onto Route 248.

35.8 km

At the stop sign, turn left to stay on Route 248.

39.6 km

When you reach the intersection of Routes 1 and 248, you will see the North River Coffee Shop. Turn right onto Route 1, a bumpy and busy main highway.

43.3 km

You will cross the North River Causeway and climb a short hill where you will turn right onto Maypoint Road.

45.1 km

At the stop sign, turn left onto Beach Grove Road.

45.9 km

At the yield sign, turn right onto North River Road.

47.0 km

At the end of North River Road, turn left onto Brighton.

47.9 km

Turn right onto Pownall Street.

48.5 km

Turn left at the third cross street off Pownall, which is Grafton Street.

48.9 km

Continue straight on Grafton Street, past the Confederation Centre of the Arts, to University Avenue and Province House, the centre of Charlottetown and the beginning of Day A and Day L. The Visitors Information Centre is straight up University Avenue on your left-hand side. The Duchess of Kent and the Charlottetown Hotel are on Kent Street, just off University Avenue, the CP Hotel is at the end of Queen Street (off Grafton Street) near the harbour, and the many tourist homes and smaller hotels are listed in the Visitors Guide. To reach Southport Trailer Park, continue on Grafton Street, cross the bridge, and take a right at your first lights after the bridge.

49.2 km

Day L

START:	Charlottetown
FINISH:	Brudenell
KM:	56.8

Today's route takes you north and east from Charlottetown to the Brudenell River via Routes 21, 22, 5, 321, and 3. You will cycle through PEI farmland along the Hillsborough River, stop to pick fresh strawberries (in season) at Goodall Strawberry Farm, visit the Government of Canada Fish Culture Station, visit the Cardigan Craft Shop, and finish your day with the option of a traditional Island lobster supper at Cardigan Lobster Suppers and theatre at Kings Playhouse in nearby Georgetown. Accommodations should be selected in the Brudenell, Georgetown, and Montague section of the Visitors Guide. The handiest campground in the vicinity is at the Brudenell River Resort, which also offers luxury hotel accommodations.

Directions

Find your way to the corner of Grafton and University, the centre of downtown Charlottetown. As you face Province House and the war memorial, turn left (east) onto Grafton Street.

0.0 km

Grafton Street will bring you to the Hillsborough Bridge, which affords an excellent view of the Charlottetown Harbour and the Hillsborough River, one of three rivers which feed the harbour. On the pylons from the old bridge to your right you can usually see hundreds of the once endangered birds, cormorants. Continue straight over the bridge, which is quite narrow and busy.

1.2 km

Immediately after the bridge you will see a highway sign which indicates Bunbury/Fort Amherst to your left. At the sign, cross the highway and turn left onto Route 21.

2.7 km

You will cross a small bridge over an inlet of the Hillsborough River. Your route continues straight.

6.7 km

As you reach a 'T' in the road at the stop sign, you will see signs indicating Route 215 to your right and Route 21 to your left. Turn left to stay on Route 21. You are headed towards Mermaid.

7.2 km

On your right you will see the Calvin Presbyterian Church, established 1830, one of hundreds of historical churches on the Island.

9.4 km

Shortly after Mermaid, you will see Kenny's Grocery on your right-hand side, one of the few grocery stores on today's route. Good place to stop for a pop and a break.

12.0 km

The Mount Ryan Sacred Heart Roman Catholic Church is on your left.

12.3 km

Just after Johnstons River there is what may appear to be a fork in the road. Stay left to stay on Route 21.

14.3 km

The recently restored Fort Augustus Church is on your right.

22.4 km

At the junction of Routes 21 and 213, you will see the Ultramar Gas and Grocery on your left. Your route continues straight on Route 21.

23.2 km

On your right you will see a sign indicating Goodall Strawberry Farm, where you can stop to pick fresh strawberries (in season). The Goodalls will provide you with baskets.

23.6 km

When you get to the end of Route 21 at the top of a short steep hill, you will be in Pisquid. Turn right onto Route 22 towards Cardigan. Look out for the railway tracks just after the turn.

28.5 km

Continue straight on Route 22 past the turn to Fanning Brook and Peakes, until you see the St. Teresa Church on your right-hand side. Stop in for a visit. It is one of the Island's most beautiful churches and worth a visit. Your route continues straight.

38.5 km

When you get to the Ultramar gas station and Quik Pik grocery store on your left, just after the signs indicating Cardigan and Route 5 to your left, you will be at the crossroads of Routes 22 and 5. Turn left onto Route 5. You are now heading towards the Government of Canada Fish Culture Station.

42.5 km

You will see Callaghan's Irving and Coffee Shop on your right-hand side.

45.8 km

When you see the Fish Culture Station on your right, you might turn onto the dirt road for a guided tour of a fish farming operation. Your route continues straight on Route 5.

50.0 km

Continue straight on Route 5, crossing Route 4 at the stop sign.

50.5 km

Shortly after crossing Route 4, you will climb a short, steep hill. The Cardigan Craft Shop is in front of you to your right.

52.3 km

Continue straight on Route 5 for 200 metres until its end at a stop sign, where you will see Cardigan Lobster Suppers, a good spot to eat. Turn right onto Route 321.

52.5 km

After you see the sign indicating Georgetown to your left via Route 3, turn left at the junction of Routes 321 and 3, onto Route 3.

54.5 km

You will cycle a few km on Route 3 before reaching Brudenell River Resort on your right. Turn right into Brudenell. The Brudenell Hotel is at the end of the road to your right, the Brudenell Campground is at the end of the road to your left. Georgetown and the Kings Playhouse are 5.4 km straight down Route 3.

56.8 km

Day M

START:	Brudenell
FINISH:	Souris
KM:	59.6

Today's route takes you north and east towards Souris via Routes 321, 311, 4, 310, and 2. Tomorrow you may board the ferry from Souris to the Magdalen Islands. You will cycle along the warm eastern shores of the Island, past Cardigan and Boughton Bay, visit the largest cattle farm on the Island—Dundas Farms, stop for a swim at Abells Cape, and visit Bay Fortune, a lobster fishing harbour and village where the Great Blue Heron congregate, particularly at low tide. Today's ride features inland farm country as well as ocean front scenery. Accommodations should be selected from the Souris and Souris West section of the Visitors Guide, with bed and breakfasts, country inns, and motels available. The nearest campground is Red Point Provincial Park, which is 13 km east of Souris on Route 16. Souris offers two excellent seafood restaurants, the Bluefin and the Platter House, both of which afford an excellent view of Colville Bay and the ocean.

Directions
Leaving the Brudenell driveway, turn left onto Route 3.

0.0

When you reach the first crossroads just past the sign indicating Morell and Cardigan, turn right onto Route 321 towards Cardigan.

2.1 km

Stay straight on this route, passing Cardigan Lobster Suppers on your right and crossing a small bridge in Cardigan, a small fishing village. On your right is a mussel farming operation in the Cardigan River. Immediately after the bridge, bear right onto Route 311 towards Woodville Mills.

4.5 km

When you see a sign to your left indicating St. Georges, you will be coming to Woodville Mills, which is at the crossroads of Routes 334 and 311. There is a dirt road in front of you. Turn left onto Route 334.

14.0 km

When you reach the end of Route 334, turn left back onto Route 311, following the sign to Primrose.

16.4 km

Continue straight on Route 311 until you reach Route 4. Turn right onto Route 4.

21.9 km

Stay on Route 4 until you see the Bridgetown Quickmart and Canteen on your right.

23.7 km

Just after the Quickmart and a small bridge is a picnic area on your left, which is a good spot for lunch.

24.0 km

Your route continues straight on Route 4 until you reach the Irving station on your right, at the corner of Routes 4 and 310. To your right, you will see a sign indicating Annandale. Turn right onto Route 310.

25.2 km

You will be cycling through Dundas Farms. Keep an eye out for the golden French-bred cattle, Charlets. At the sign to Bay Fortune and Annandale, stay left towards Bay Fortune to continue on Route 310.

34.6 km

Continue on Route 310 until you see the Saint Francis Roman Catholic Church on your left-hand side, where you will bear left to stay on Route 310.

36.3 km

At the fork in road, stay right on Route 310.

40.2 km

Continue straight until you see a small bay in front of you, at the bottom of a short, steep hill; this is Bay Fortune. If you follow the access road on your right for a few hundred metres, you will come to a lobster fishing harbour and canning operation. The dirt road, also on your right, takes you to the warm and beautiful beach of Abells Cape, surrounded by the Island's trademark red sandstone cliffs. At approximately two o'clock in the afternoon, you can catch a glimpse of the *Lucy Maud Montgomery*, the ferry to the Magdalens. Your route continues straight on Route 310.

44.2 km

Follow Route 310 through the crossroads of Routes 310 and 340 until you reach Route 2. Turn right onto Route 2 and cycle the last 8.4 km to Souris.

49.3 km

On your left you will see the St. Alexis Church.

53.8 km

On your right just before the bridge over Colville Bay is the Platter House.

56.9 km

On your right just after the bridge is a Visitor Information Centre.

57.7 km

Continue straight through Souris on Main Street (Route 2) until you see the Hilltop Motel, an inexpensive and well-maintained motel. The Red Point Provincial Park is 13 km straight up Route 16, which Route 2 has now become. The turnoff to the Magdalen Islands ferry terminal is to your right down Knights Avenue.

59.6 km

Day N

START:	Souris
FINISH:	Cap-aux-Meules
KM:	1.1 km (cycling)
	134 km (ferry)

Today's travel is a few short kilometres of cycling and five hours on the *Lucy Maud Montgomery* ferry to the Magdalen Islands. Between April 1st and June 20th, the ferry leaves Souris every day at 2:00 p.m., Mondays excepted. From June 21st to September 15, it leaves every day at 2:00 p.m., Tuesdays excepted, when it leaves at 2:00 a.m. (Wednesday morning). From September 16th to

September 30th, it leaves every day at 2:00 p.m., Mondays excepted. 1989 prices are $25.00 per adult one way and $5.75 for a bicycle. Prices usually go up about five percent per year. For travel and weather information (trips are sometimes cancelled due to bad seas) phone (902) 687-2181. This is a local Souris number so you need not use the area code if you are in Souris.

As you will most likely be leaving at 2:00 p.m., you could use your morning to cycle north up to the East Point Lighthouse via Route 16. (The end of Day M is the beginning of Route16, the Red Point Provincial Park is on Route 16.) If you go, you should visit the Basin Head Fisheries Museum along the way. Be mindful of the time as this morning jaunt is 52 km there and back. If you are staying at the Red Point Provincial Park, you are 13 km from the ferry terminal, so factor in your departure time accordingly.

Directions

Starting at the end point of Day M with the Hilltop Motel on your left and Knights Avenue on your right, turn right onto Knights Avenue. You will cross a small bridge, turn left, then right and arrive at the ferry terminal. You may buy your tickets at the building to your right. Cyclists may walk on when the ferry arrives; you need not wait in line with cars.

1.1 km

The trip to the Magdalens will take five hours, and along the way you may enjoy traditional bands, singing, and dancing in the bars, dine in one of two restaurants, or keep a lookout for whales and seals from the observation decks. During the last half-hour of your trip, keep an eye out for Entry Island and your first view of the stark, treeless, often mist-enshrouded Magdalen Islands.

134 km (ferry trip)

When you disembark from the ferry, cycle up to Chemin Principal, which is the end of the ferry access road. On your left is the Magdalen Islands Tourist Information

Office. The nearest campground is the Camping Gros-Cap, which is 5.2 km to your left. Follow Chemin Principal until you reach Chemin de Gros-Cap, where you will turn left. At your first paved left, turn left off Chemin de Gros-Cap. Camping Gros-Cap is 200 metres from the turn on your right.

A favourite hotel is the Hôtel Au Vieux Couvent, a restored historic convent which features an excellent French restaurant, a jazz bar in the basement, and a patio restaurant which overlooks the ocean. It is 5.3 km from the ferry terminal. To get there, turn right on Chemin Principal and stay straight on this road, crossing a bridge (where it becomes Route 199), passing Le P'tite Café Restaurant and an Irving station on your left until you see a large stone building at a turn in the road: this is the Hôtel Au Viex Couvent.

All routes layed out in this guide will start from the Tourist Information Office near the ferry terminal, so just retrace your steps tomorrow. Your accommodations will likely be no more than twenty minutes away by bicycle. It is recommended that you stay at the same accommodations for the few days you will be on the Magdalens. As the Islands are quite small, you can cycle daily from accommodations near Cap-aux-Meules to most destinations and easily be back by the end of the day.

135.1 km

Day O

START:	Cap-aux-Meules
FINISH:	Cap-aux-Meules
KM:	72.0

Today's route takes you to the artisan village of La Grave, the Isthmus of Île aux Ouefs, where you will see beach front on both sides of the road, and have spectacular views of blue herons and thousands of migratory birds on Gull Island. Most of your day will follow Route 199. In La Grave, you'll see traditional artisan shops, the Musée de la Mer, and enjoy lunch at a French cafe.

Directions:

Starting with the Tourist Information Office on your left-hand side and Chemin Principal in front of you, turn right onto Chemin Principal.

0.0 km

You will pass Chemin du Marconi on your left before you reach Chemin des Caps, where you will turn left onto Chemin des Caps.

0.8 km

At Chemin de L'hospital, turn left at the fork in the road to stay on Chemin des Caps. In front of you, you will see the Dune du Nord.

3.2 km

On your right, you will see the grocery store Magasin des Aubaines Familliales.

3.4 km

Coming up on your left is the Eglise Fatima, a sea shell-shaped Roman Catholic Church.

4.3 km

Your next landmark is the Depanneur Chevarie (a general store) on your right.

5.9 km

At the Chemin de Huets, turn left for a short detour to Ateliers Art-Gil Pottery and Ceramics. Your route continues straight on Chemin des Caps.

6.6 km

At Chemin de la Belle Anse, turn right where you see the sign Belle Anse.

6.9 km

A good stop is at the sharp corner in the road where the two arrow signs are. The shore is spectacular.

7.9 km

When you reach the end of Chemin de la Belle Anse, turn right onto Chemin des Caps.

8.6 km

The roadside restaurant Casse Croute aux Elores is on your left, an excellent spot for a snack. You are now entering L'Étang du Nord.

9.0 km

As you approach the bottom of the hill you are now on, keep an eye out for your next turn onto Chemin du Phare. You will see a blue house on your left. Turn right onto Chemin du Phare.

10.0 km

When you reach the beach, stay right to go up a dirt road to the lighthouse for a spectacular view, where the cover picture of this guide was taken.

10.8 km

Return the way you came and back onto Chemin du Phares. Continue on Chemin du Phare until you reach Chemin des Caps. Turn right onto Chemin des Caps.

12.3 km

Turn right at the end of Chemin des Caps (at the stop sign) onto Chemin L'Étang du Nord.

13.5 km

Your next landmark on your left is the Co-op Sociale, a grocery store.

13.9 km

Turn left at the end of Chemin L'Étang du Nord at the stop sign, onto Chemin Boisville.

14.0 km

Turn right onto Chemin Delaney.

14.5 km

At the Pepsi sign (Depaneur A.Y. Boudreau) turn right onto Chemin Molaison.

17.7 km

At the end of Chemin Molaison, turn left onto Chemin Coloumb.

18.4 km

Your next turn is a quick right onto Chemin Chiasson.

18.7 km

At the end of Chemin Chiasson, turn right onto Chemin Martinique.

20.0 km

After the marsh area and long bridge, stay left at the fork, following signs to Havre Aubert via Route 199 ouest.

34.9 km

Continue straight on Route 199 ouest until you reach Graves, an excellent spot for lunch, to visit the seaside artisan shops, and stop by the Musée de la Mer. Café de la Grave is on your left.

39.4 km

After lunch your route continues back the way you came on Route 199 ouest.

39.4 km

When you reach the fork in the road at the ESSO station, stay right on Route 199 est.

45.2 km

Follow Route 199 est back onto Île du Cap aux Meules for the next 20.3 km until you reach Chemin de la Pré, which is 2.0 km after the John Deere sign on your left. Turn right onto Chemin de la Pré.

62.3 km

At the end of Chemin de la Pré, at the stop sign, turn onto Chemin de Gros-Cap. If you are staying at Camping Gros-Cap, it is 1.2 k.m down the road.

66.2 km

Continue on Chemin Gros-Cap until you reach Chemin Principal, which is Route 199 est and follow it until you reach the Tourist Information Office. Hôtel Au Vieux Couvent is 5.3 km further along Route 199 est.

72.0 km

Day P

Start:	Cap-aux-Meules
Finish:	Cap-aux-Meules
Km:	84.0

Today's route takes you along flat, untravelled roads towards Île Rouge, Pointe-aux-Loups, les Meines Seleine, Dune du Nord Beach, and Grosse-Île via Route 199 est. You will cycle along a thin isthmus, with both shores visible during most of the day. Because this route is open to both shores, it is usually quite windy. Along the way you will see wind generators—by which the Magdalen Islands generates much of its power, Dune du Sud, a glass blowing artisan, Dune du Nord, and have lunch in Grosse Île. There are not many directions today as you are cycling straight out one road and back. Consequently, you could easily shorten your route if you wish.

Directions
Starting at the Tourist Information office, turn right onto Chemin Principal, which is also Route 199 est.

0.0 km

As you reach a short, steep hill, you will see Le Pedalo boat rentals on your left, a good way to tour the bay, Lagune du Havre aux Maisons.

2.0 km

After you cross the bridge you will be on Havre aux Maisons. On your left is a lobster pound and mussel farm, an inexpensive and traditional way to buy your supper, perhaps on your way back this afternoon.

3.3 km

Just beyond the Irving Station, you will see Le P'tite Café on your left, an excellent, intimate French restaurant.

4.9 km

In front of you at the curve in the road is the Hôtel au Vieux Couvent, where you may want to stop for a snack at their ocean view patio restaurant. Your route continues on Route 199 est.

5.3 km

As you reach Place du Dune du Sud, you will see the Restaurant Motel Theriault on your left.

10.8 km

Your next landmark is a series of wind generators on your right. By now you will probably appreciate why they are situated on this route.

16.2 km

As you cross the bridge over Lagune de la Grande Entrée, you will have spectacular views of the Dune du Nord and Dune du Sud, in front of you and behind you. Shortly after the bridge on Dune du Nord is the Dune du Nord Beach. This beach extends as far as the eye can see, and is usually quite empty. Currents can be strong here, so do not swim out too far.

17.8 km

The next community you reach will be Pointe-aux-Loups, an oasis in the middle of Dune du Nord. Fresh clams and mussels are sold on the roadside here. You may want to visit the harbour, go for a swim at the public beach, or stop at Action Plus, the grocery store on your left.

24.1 km

Your next landmark is Les Meines Seleine (salt mines), on your right. Salt mining is one of the major industries on the Magdelens.

39.8 km

When you reach the causeway, you will see an Irving station, just after which is your best spot for lunch at the Country Kitchen Gros Îles.

42.0 km

As you may have noticed, today's route followed Route 199 est from start to finish. To return to the beginning of today's route, simply turn around and retrace your steps along Route 199 ouest until you reach the Tourist Information Office.

84.0 km

Day Q

Start:	Cap-aux-Meules
Finish:	Brudenell
Km:	134 km (Ferry)
	68.5 km (cycling

Today's travel is by return ferry to Souris, PEI, where you cycle back to Brudenell via two fishing harbours, Naufrage and St. Peters, and down through central Kings County. Once on PEI, you will be following Routes 358, 306, 16, 313, 4, 5, 321, and 3. During 1989, from April 1 to June 20 and September 16 to September 30, the ferry left every day at 8:00 a.m., Mondays excepted. From June 21 to September 15 it left every day at 8:00 a.m., Tuesdays excepted, when it left at 8:00 p.m. Please check the schedule for the current year. The trip is about five hours long, and as you will most likely be leaving at 8:00 a.m., you should arrive in Souris at 1:00 p.m. You should eat lunch on the ferry so that you start cycling immediately upon arrival on the Island, as you have 68.5 km to cycle. Accommodations should be selected in the Brudenell, Georgetown and Montague section of the Visitors Guide. The handiest campground in the vicinity is at the Brudenell River Resort, which also offers luxury hotel accommodations. Both campers and hotel guests have access to all facilities, including a shuttle bus to the Kings Playhouse in Georgetown, 5.4 km away.

Directions (from Souris ferry terminal)

Find your way back up to Main Street in Souris via Knights Avenue from the ferry terminal and turn left onto Main Street. Follow Main Street to the outskirts of Souris. Just before the causeway, take your last paved right onto Route 358. You will see the Ocean View Restaurant on your right-hand side.

1.7 km

When you reach the stop sign, just after the sign indicating Souris River, turn left to stay on Route 358.

2.4 km

Follow Route 358 until its end, just after the sign to New Zealand. Turn right at the stop sign onto Route 306.

7.7 km

Your next landmark is Whalen's Grocery on your right.

10.7 km

Route 306 ends at Route 16 just after the sign to St. Margarets. Turn left at the stop sign onto Route 16.

16.6 km

Coming up on your right is St. Margarets of Scotland Roman Catholic Church.

20.5 km

The next stop for supplies/snacks is the Little Store and Irving station.

21.9 km

When you cross a small bridge over Cow Creek, you will be able to see Naufrage Harbour on your right.

24.7 km

A detour to Naufrage Harbour is the next paved road on your right. Naufrage Harbour is worth a visit and occasionally sponsors Summer Fiddling Festivals and concerts. Today's route continues straight on Route 16.

24.9 km

The next landmark is St. Peters, one of the Island's large fishing communities. In front of you to your left you will see the Bayview Corner Store, to your right is the St. Peters Bay Bridge. Cross the bridge onto Route 313.

41.1 km

Continue on Route 313 through inland Kings County farm country until you reach Route 4, just after the sign to Montague. Turn right onto Route 4, a busy road.

60.9 km

After the sign to Cardigan, turn left onto Route 5.

62.3 km

After you climb a short, steep hill, you will see the Cardigan Craft Shop in front of you to your right.

64.0 km

Continue on Route 5 for 200 metres until it ends at a stop sign, where you will see Cardigan Lobster Suppers, a good spot for supper. Turn right onto Route 321.

64.2 km

After you see the sign indicating Georgetown to your left via Route 3, turn left at the junction of Routes 321 and 3 onto Route 3.

66.3 km

You will cycle a few kilometres on Route 3 before reaching Brudenell River Resort on your right. Turn right into Brudenell. The Brudenell Hotel is at the end of the road to your right, the Brudenell Campground is at the

end of the road to your left. Georgetown and the Kings
Playhouse is 5.4 km straight down Route 3.

68.5 km

Day R

START: Brudenell
FINISH: Murray River
KM: 59.5

Today's route follows the southeastern shoreline of the
Island via Routes 3, 4, and 17. You will be passing through
Montague, St. Marys Bay, St. Andrews Point (where you
can stop for a quiet picnic lunch beside a remote
lighthouse), Panmure Island Provincial Park, Point
Pleasant and Murray Harbour, before arriving in Murray
River. The only accommodations in Murray River is the
Countryman Bed and Breakfast, which is listed in the
Visitors Guide under Murray River. The nearest
campground is the Gladstone Tent and Trailer Park, 2 km
east of Murray River on Route 348.

Directions
At the end of the Brudenell River Resort driveway, turn
left onto Route 3.

0.0 km

At the junction of Routes 3 and 4, turn left onto Route 4.

5.7 km

As you arrive in Montague, the largest town on today's
route, you will see the Church of Christ on your
right-hand side. Montague has a number of grocery
stores, a good place to buy supplies and food for a picnic
lunch at St. Andrews Point, coming up in 11.9 km.

10.3 km

Continue straight through Montague, crossing the bridge over Montague River.

11.3 km

As you reach the outskirts of Montague, continue straight; you should now be on Route 17.

11.4 km

Coming up is the turnoff for St. Andrews Point. This is an easy turn to miss. Look for the sign to Lower Montague and St. Andrews Point Lighthouse. Turn left.

16.5 km

When you reach Lower Montague, stay left at the fork in the road towards St. Andrews Point.

18.8 km

Continue on the road as it changes to a dirt road until you reach a cliffside clearing overlooking Georgetown, the Harbour and Panmure Island. Enjoy your lunch.

22.2 km

Your route continues back the way you came until you come to your first left after the sign to Albion and Sturgeon. Turn left back towards Route 17.

25.6 km

At the stop sign, turn left onto Route 17 towards Albion and Sturgeon.

26.5 km

Your next landmark is the Sturgeon United Church on your left.

33.6 km

You will see the Laurie McHerron general store on your right.

39.9 km

Murray Harbour Presbyterian Church is on your left.

44.4 km

When you see Johnston's in front of you, keep right to stay on Route 17.

47.5 km

Just after the Murray River sign, at the junction of Routes 17A and 17, turn left to stay on Route 17.

48.1 km

After the bridge, stay right on the paved road, Route 17.

52.5 km

At the intersection of Routes 4 and 17, turn left towards Murray River.

56.8 km

As you arrive in Murray River, you will come to a stop sign, which is the junction of Routes 17 and 24. This is the end of Day R and the starting point of Day S. The Countrymen Bed and Breakfast is on School Street. To get to the Gladstone Tent and Trailer Park, turn left at the stop sign, cycle through Murray River, and turn right onto Route 348.

59.5 km

Day S

Start:	Murray River
Finish:	Charlottetown
Km:	62.5

Today's route takes you west through inland farm country and back to Charlottetown via Routes 24, 3, 216, 215, 21 and 1. You will see many of the Island's corporate farming operations, with processing and packing plants on their properties, pass through Vernon River, home of the Garden Restaurant, where a colony of swans inhabit a nearby pond. While your morning route, Route 24, is realtively untavelled, cars do travel at high speeds along this route, so be sure to cycle carefully. You will cycle over some of the larger hills on the Island, but none of them should take you more than fifteen minutes to climb. Accommodtions should be selected from the Charlottetown section of the Visitors Guide. The two luxury hotels in Charlottetown are the Charlottetown Hotel and the CP Hotel; a favourite small hotel is the Duchess of Kent, with inexpensive, clean, beautifully antique-furnished rooms. It is almost always full, so be sure to book ahead. The nearest campground to Charlottetown is the Southport Trailer Park. To get there, follow Grafton Street to the Hillsborough Bridge, cross the bridge and turn right on Stratford Road.

Directions

Starting at the end point of Day R, the junction of Routes 17 and 24, head out on Route 24 towards Vernon River. The Murray River United Church will be on your right.

0.0 km

When you reach the stop sign at the junction of Routes 24 and 324, turn left to stay on Route 24.

6.9 km

When you reach the junction of Routes 315 and 24, continue straight on Route 24. If you are coming from, or planning to go to, Nova Scotia via Northumberland ferries, follow Route 315 to Wood Islands. (Directions to and from both ferries are detailed after *Day V* in the Daily Itineraries.) Otherwise, continue straight on Route 24 towards Vernon River.

11.3 km

When you reach the end of Route 24 at Route 3 in Vernon River, turn left onto Route 3, a busy route.

31.6 km

Turn right just after the sign to Hermitage/Avondale onto Route 216.

32.0 km

Just after the sign indicating Mount Albion to your left, turn left onto Route 5 at the junction of Routes 5 and 216.

36.4 km

Stay straight on Route 5 past Elliottvale until you reach Avondale. At the crossroads, continue straight through to stay on Route 5. When you get to what *appears* to be the end of Route 5 at Clarkin (where Route 213 crosses in front of you), take a quick right and then a quick left to get back on Route 5. Continue straight on Route 5.

40.7 km

The next turn is easy to miss. Look for a sign indicating Bethel via Route 215. Turn right on 215, which is partially unpaved. If you reach Route 1 at the Irving station, you have gone too far, and can retrace your steps a few hundred metres back to Route 215.

47.5 km

At the stop sign in Bethel, turn left to stay on Route 215.

49.6 km

Continue straight on Route 215 until you reach Mount Herbert at the stop sign and intersection of Route 21. Turn right onto Route 21.

54.7 km

When you reach the Glen Stewart School on your right, turn left at the intersection to stay on Route 21 towards Bunbury.

55.8 km

Follow Route 21 to the intersection of Route 1, where you will see the Hillsborough Bridge to your right. Turn right onto Route 1.

60.2 km

Cross the Hillsborough Bridge onto Grafton Street and stay straight on Grafton Street until you reach University Avenue, and the end of Day S.

62.5 km

Three Day Loop through New Brunswick and Nova Scotia

If you wish to complement your cycling routes with a three-day tour through New Brunswick and Nova Scotia, use the following directions. This part of Nova Scotia and New Brunswick is quite flat, similar to the terrain in PEI. Kilometre by kilometre notation is not provided. The three-day tour will take you from the Cape Tormentine, New Brunswick ferry terminal to the Caribou, Nova Scotia ferry terminal, both of which offer ferry service to PEI. The connection routes from the PEI tours to the PEI ferry terminals are detailed at the end of Day V. The traffic in New Brunswick and Nova Scotia is heavier than in PEI. To make reservations at most accommo-dations and campgrounds throughout Nova Scotia, you should phone one of the following toll-free numbers:

From Nova Scotia, New Brunswick, and PEI:
   1-800-565-7105

From Quebec, Labrador or Newfoundland:
   1-800-565-7180

From Central or Southern Ontario: 1-800-565-7140

From Northern Ontario, and the West: 1-800-565-7166

From the continental USA (except Maine):
   1-800-341-6096

From Maine: 1-800-492-0643

Day T

Start:	Cape Tormentine, N.B.
Finish:	Amherst, N.S.
Km:	Approx. 68

Today's route leaves from the New Brunswick side of the Marine Atlantic ferry, a forty-five minute trip which leaves Borden, PEI every hour on the half-hour during the day, starting at 6:30 a.m. You will cycle along the southeastern shore of New Brunswick near Baie Verte until you reach Amherst, Nova Scotia, a couple of kilometres across the provincial borders. Your route follows Routes 960, 16, and 366 into Amherst. There are two motels, one inn, one guest home and three campgrounds available in the Amherst area. As today's route connects up from Day J and Day D of the PEI Daily Itineraries, you may want to spend the night in Victoria-by-the-Sea. Victoria-by-the-Sea is only a few kilometres from the Day J and Day D turnoff to the New Brunswick ferry. Keep in mind that today's total distance is measured from the New Brunswick ferry terminal.

Directions
Starting from km 96.7 of Day J or km 29.4 of Day D, follow the connection route to Borden, PEI, which is detailed after Day V in this guide. From Cape Tormentine, New Brunswick follow Route 960 until you reach Route 16, then turn left onto Route 16. Follow Route 16 until you reach Port Elgin, where you will turn left, following the signs to Baie Verte and Tidnish, Nova Scotia. When you reach the Nova Scotia border, turn right onto Route 366, heading southwest. Follow Route 366 until you reach Route 6 west, which will take you into Amherst.

Approx. 68 km

Day U

Start:	Amherst
Finish:	Tatamagouche
Km:	Approx. 82

Today's route follows the Sunrise Trail via Route 6 east, along the northwestern shore of Nova Scotia. You will pass many supervised beaches along the warm waters of the Northumberland Strait. A good bet for a lunch stop is Pugwash, where the Gathering of the Scottish Clans takes place on July 1 of every year. Pugwash is also the site of the yearly Thinkers' Conference, a meeting of Soviet Bloc and Western scientists, sponsored by the late American railroad magnate, Cyrus Eaton. In Tatamagouche, you may stay either at the Brule Shore Cabins (the only accommodations) or the Nelson Memorial Park and Campground. If you cannot secure reservations at either spot, you can stop in Wallace, about twenty-five km before Tatamagouche on Route 6 east. Wallace offers a greater selection of accommodations.

Directions
Follow Route 6 east, also known as the Sunrise Trail, until you reach Tatamagouche. In Tatamagouche, you should visit the Sunrise Trail Museum, which highlights the history of this area of Nova Scotia.

Approx. 82 km.

Day V

Start: Tatamagouche
Finish: Wood Islands, PEI
Km: Approx. 56

Today's route follows more of the Sunrise Trail, along the north central shore of Nova Scotia, until you reach Caribou, Nova Scotia, where the ferry leaves hourly to Wood Islands, PEI. You will again spend much of the day cycling along the Northumberland Strait shoreline via Routes 6 east and 106 north. The ferry will take seventy-five minutes to cross to Wood Islands, PEI. Tomorrow your route will connect up at km 11.3 of Day S on the Island. To get to this portion of Day S, follow the connecting route from the Wood Island ferry terminal detailed at the end of Day V. Accommodations should be selected from the Wood Islands, Wood Islands East, and Wood Islands West section of the Visitors Guide. The only campground available is the Northumberland Provincial Park, on Route 4, three km east of the ferry terminal.

Directions

Leaving Tatamagouche, follow Route 6 east along the north shore until you reach Route 106, where you will turn left onto Route 106. Follow Route 106 until you reach the Caribou ferry terminal. Along the way you will pass through Pictou, where Scottish emigration to Nova Scotia began in 1773.

Approx. 56 km

<hr>

Connecting Routes to
New Brunswick and Nova Scotia ferries

<hr>

The following connectors hook up with routes outlined in the Daily Itineraries, are part of some of the Recommended Tours, and are useful if you are coming to the Island by bicycle.

•   Maritime Atlantic (Borden, PEI to Cape Tormentine, New Brunswick):

Going to the Borden ferry terminal: Leaving from km 29.4 on Day D, or km 96.7 on Day J from the Daily Itineraries section of this guide, turn right at the intersection of Routes 10 and 1, onto Route 1 west. Follow Route 1 until you reach the Borden ferry terminal.

3.2 km

Coming from the Borden ferry terminal: Leaving from the ferry terminal, follow Route 1 east until you reach the intersection of Routes 1 and 10. You will see an Irving station on your left. Turn right onto Route 10 to follow the rest of Day D's itinerary from km 29.4. It is 18.1 km to Victoria-by-the-Sea, a good place to spend the night.

3.2 km

- Northumberland ferries (Wood Islands, PEI to Caribou, Nova Scotia):

Going to the Wood Islands ferry terminal: Leaving from km 11.3 of Day S of the Daily Itineraries section of this guide, turn left at the junction of Routes 315 and 24 onto Route 315. Follow Route 315 until you reach the intersection of Routes 4, 1, and 315. Go straight through on Route 1 east until you reach the Wood Islands ferry terminal.

12.9 km

Coming from the Wood Islands ferry terminal: Leaving from the ferry terminal on Route 1 east, follow Route 1 until you reach the intersection of Routes 4, 1, and 315. Go straight through on Route 315 until you reach the intersection of Route 315 and 24. Turn left onto Route 24, and follow the rest of Day S's itinerary from km 11.3

12.9 km

CYCLING TOUR COMPANIES
IN THE MARITIMES

As of 1989, there were four major package cycling tour companies which offer package tours of the Maritime provinces. Cycling clubs and associations also run some tours and offer maps of cycling routes. They vary in the type of cyclist they cater to, some being more geared towards the experienced cyclist, others to beginners. Generally, package tours are fully pre-arranged cycling vacations, usually under ten days in length. One fee includes most meals, accommodations, some activities, one or two tour guides, and a support van which carries your luggage. An additional fee can be paid for bicycle and equipment rental. Groups are usually limited to fifteen and prices are based on double occupancy. Transportation to and from the starting point is not included.

Package Cycling Tour Companies

Down East Bicycle Tours offers six day tours of Nova Scotia as well as tours to Newfoundland and Bermuda. Run by enigmatic George Dagley and his family, *Down East Bicycle Tours* has a good reputation through the cycling network as an enthusiastic and personal tour operation.

For more information:

Down East Bicycle Tours
Comp. 41, R.R. # 2 Kingston, Nova Scotia
Canada B0P 1R0
(902) 765-8923   In Maine 1-800-492-0643
USA 1-800-341-6096

Freewheeling Bicycle Adventures offers five separate tours of Nova Scotia during the summer months, ranging from five-day to ten-day tours. They usually stay in country inns and base their tours mostly out of Halifax. They also offer comprehensive tour planning of different involvement, where they will assist you in putting together your own vacation.

> **Freewheeling Bicycle Adventures**
> R.R. 1
> Boutilier's Point, Nova Scotia B0G 1G0
> (902) 826-2437   (902) 826-7541

Maine Coast Cyclers offers six-day tours to Prince Edward Island on five dates throughout the summer. They also offer tours to the northeastern United States. They stay at country inns and cater to the more independent cyclist. Their clientele tends to head out on long rides, often on different routes, with the whole group getting together at night. Their tour guides are usually highly experienced cyclists, often having racing backgrounds.

> **Maine Coast Cyclers**
> P.O. Box 1234
> Camden, Maine USA 04842
> (802) 496-4603 (before June 1)
> (207) 236-8608 (after June 1)

Sunset Bicycle Tours runs sixteen tours of Prince Edward Island and the Magdalen Islands every summer, with tours leaving every week. It also runs tours to Crete and Ireland. The Prince Edward Island and Magdalen Island tours are five and nine days respectively. Participants stay at resort hotels, and have activities such as theatre, horseback riding on the beach, sailing, deep-sea fishing, and lobster suppers included. Most of their tour guides are Island residents and tend to be highly service oriented, staying with their groups during all cycling and nighttime activities.

> **Sunset Bicycle Tours**
> 455 University Avenue
> Charlottetown, PEI C1A 4N8
> (902) 892-0606

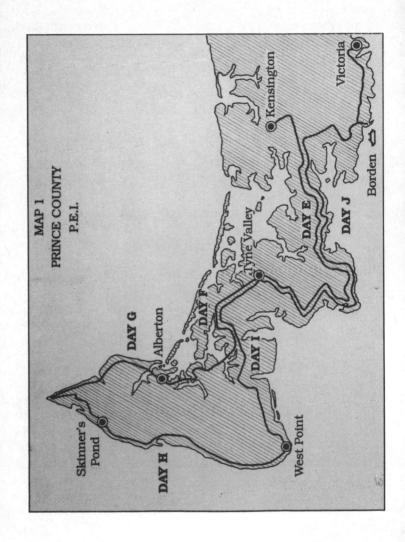

MAP 1
PRINCE COUNTY
P.E.I.

DAY G

DAY H

Skinner's Pond

Alberton

DAY F

DAY I

West Point

Tyne Valley

DAY E

DAY J

Kensington

Victoria

Borden

95

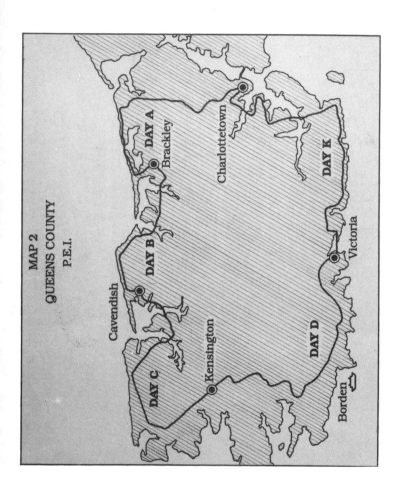

MAP 2
QUEENS COUNTY
P.E.I.

Cavendish

Brackley

Charlottetown

DAY A

DAY B

DAY K

DAY C

Kensington

Victoria

DAY D

Borden

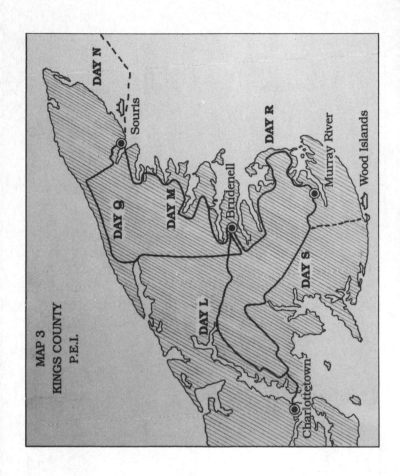

MAP 3
KINGS COUNTY
P.E.I.

DAY N

Souris

DAY 9

DAY M

Brudenell

DAY R

Murray River

Wood Islands

DAY L

DAY S

Charlottetown

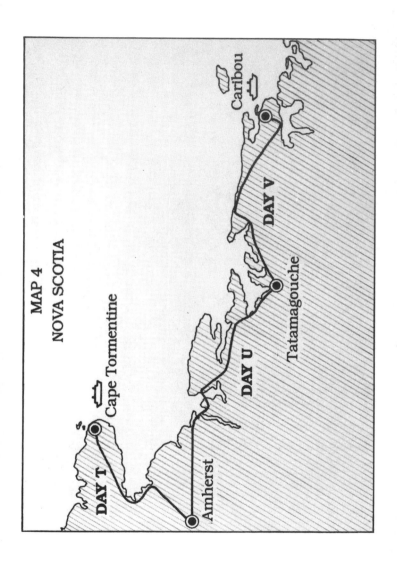

MAP 4
NOVA SCOTIA

Cape Tormentine

Caribou

DAY T

DAY U

DAY V

Amherst

Tatamagouche

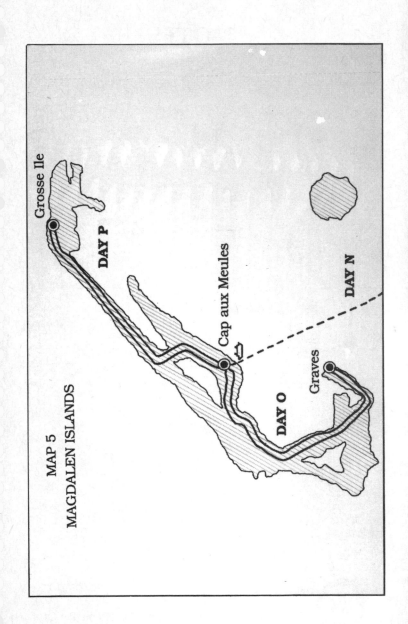

MAP 5
MAGDALEN ISLANDS

Grosse Ile

DAY P

Cap aux Meules

DAY O

DAY N

Graves

NOTES

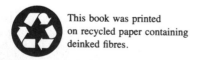

This book was printed
on recycled paper containing
deinked fibres.

Printed in Canada